T0330302

Real Estate Development and Investment

Founded in 1807, John Wiley & Sons is the oldest independent publishing company in the United States. With offices in North America, Europe, Australia and Asia, Wiley is globally committed to developing and marketing print and electronic products and services for our customers' professional and personal knowledge and understanding.

The Wiley Finance series contains books written specifically for finance and investment professionals as well as sophisticated individual investors and their financial advisors. Book topics range from portfolio management to e-commerce, risk management, financial engineering, valuation and financial instrument analysis, as well as much more.

For a list of available titles, please visit our Web site at www.Wiley Finance.com.

Real Estate Development and Investment

A Comprehensive Approach

STEPHEN P. PECA

WILEY

John Wiley & Sons, Inc.

Published by John Wiley & Sons, Inc., Hoboken, New Jersey.
Published simultaneously in Canada.

For general information on our other products and services or for technical support, please contact our Customer Care Department within the United States at (800) 762-2974, outside the United States at (317) 572-3993 or fax (317) 572-4002.

Wiley also publishes its books in a variety of electronic formats. Some content that appears in print may not be available in electronic books. For more information about Wiley products, visit our web site at www.wiley.com.

Library of Congress Cataloging-in-Publication Data:

Peca, Stephen P.
  Real estate development and investment: a comprehensive approach/Stephen P. Peca.
    p.   cm. — (Wiley finance series)
  Includes index.
  ISBN 978-0-470-22308-6 (cloth)
  1. Real estate development.   2. Real estate investment.   II. Title.
  HD1390.P43   2009
  333.33—dc22   2008047052

10 9 8 7 6 5 4 3 2 1

Contents

Preface

I have been involved in the real estate industry and development business in one aspect or another now for 30 years. I was trained as a CPA, went to law school for a year, was an accountant, was a chief financial officer, have been part of several development teams, was a commercial banker, was an investment banker, and now am an entrepreneur and a teacher. While these roles seem to be disjointed and unrelated, they are not. Virtually all of my roles have been focused on the real estate industry, with a brief departure into corporate banking and project finance. When I started in real estate development, very few academic programs were available to teach people about the business. I was trained, just like everyone else in the industry, by on-the-job training. Today, there are many more academic programs—even internationally—proving the demand for the knowledge.

This book provides a systematic and practical analysis of the phases of the real estate development process, including conceptualization, site acquisition, planning and design, the construction process, financing, and leasing and marketing, followed by investment management. The linear process I have outlined for you, the reader, will help you pursue your first real estate development or redevelopment project, or help the experienced person refine the process he or she has been using. This book, at the very least, will perhaps help you look at real estate development from an entirely different perspective. The book addresses details of the development process, but does not get so detailed as to address the fine points of each area of the development process, and, as a result, is highly readable.

Being a developer, the leader of the development process, requires experience and thought. I try to scatter the book with quotes from famous and not-so-famous people that should help the reader gain a philosophic understanding of the topics.

I have been teaching a course on the real estate development process for more than five years at a major university. This book offers an all-inclusive approach; that is, many developers simply focus on the financial or construction aspects of development and give only passing reference to the other—and no less important—aspects of the development process, such as idea refinement, branding, or investment management.

Frankly, real estate development and investment, while exciting and sexy, is still viewed as an odd investment type. Major changes have occurred over the years, such as institutional investors directly investing in real estate development projects in the 1990s. So, real estate is now considered a solid alternative investment. Hedge funds are investing in real estate projects. Private equity firms are investing in real estate. So real estate has finally come into its own. But many still think there is a mysterious element to the business and process. I think the mystery is because the essential way to obtain the knowledge is still by on-the-job training and experience. Even as students complete my course on the subject, they have the motivation, they have the knowledge, and now they have to actually go do it.

What I hope to accomplish in this book is to impart my knowledge and experience to the reader. I will try to get you to think differently when approaching a real estate development. Let me point out here that when I am saying real estate development, I am talking about ground-up development, renovation, brownfield development, and everything in between. Thus, this book should be of interest not only to the active real estate developer—new or experienced—but also to the institutional investors, hedge funds, private equity firms, commercial banks, and investment banks that are trying to understand the industry so they can make better investments or understand their clients' activities.

Leadership, management and control of the development team, and public-private partnerships are featured issues. The book will take readers through the development process from historical considerations to financial feasibility to asset disposition by using a number of illustrations and anecdotes. Each chapter finishes with a section on learning points, things that you should understand after reading each chapter.

Useful to all readers is that once you understand the overall development process, you can pursue development anywhere in the world. Yes, the laws are different, but the laws are different everywhere—New York, Des Moines, Beijing, or Kabul—yet the development process is exactly the same. So my aim is for you to learn the entire development process, learn a way of thinking, and use this book as a reference as you pursue your exciting career or business in real estate development anywhere in the world. Additionally, no matter what the state of the economy might be in a given geographic location, following the development process as I have outlined it will almost always result in a successful development project.

Overall, this book has the following learning objectives for readers:

■ **Understand the key steps in the development process:** A key to successful development is following a standard path from the beginning to the end. A developer faces many tangential issues that need to be addressed, but a developer must have this set path in mind throughout the development process to be successful.

- **Appreciate factors affecting the demand for different land uses and development:** Demand does not arise from studying and interpreting marketing data. Demand often starts as subjective beliefs derived from intuition and common sense.
- **Appreciate the need for universal, current, and broad knowledge:** Everything a developer reads, hears, or sees is relevant to the development process. It is this universal, current information that gives a developer hints or suggestions for a planned real estate project.
- **Appreciate key legal issues that must be considered by real estate developers:** Everything—everything—a developer does involves a contract: buying property, selling property, leasing property, financing property, everything.
- **Appreciate the importance of environmental considerations in real estate development:** Environmental consideration here is not limited to environmental contamination. It is true that environmental contamination must be addressed, but real estate development also causes change to the surrounding community environment. That is, when any project is developed—ground-up or regeneration—that development causes change to the surrounding community or environment. It is important to understand what that change is and address it proactively, just as a developer would address environmental contamination proactively.
- **Understand the role of the different professionals and companies involved in the development process:** Myriad professionals and companies get involved in a real estate development project. The specific types and numbers vary greatly, but a key responsibility of developers is to identify requisite professionals and companies to assist them in the development process.
- **Develop an appreciation for the importance of ethics in the development process:** Ethics is critical in real estate development. A developer's reputation is paramount for becoming successful in this field. Having a reputation for practicing good ethics often helps a developer through the entire development process. We have all heard about six degrees of separation; I believe that in the real estate industry, it's more like two degrees of separation.
- **Learn the interaction of market research, financing, planning, legal considerations, contract negotiation, design, construction, marketing, leasing, and property management:** This point describes the difficulty of

being a developer. Being a developer does not require substantial knowledge or education; it is not rocket science. What is exceedingly difficult, however, is keeping everyone on your development team on track, doing what they are supposed to do when they are supposed to be doing it. This coordination or project management can be very difficult.

Acknowledgments

Many people and experiences have contributed to my overall background in the commercial real estate industry. I suppose it all started in the late 1970s, when I joined Urban Investment & Development Co. The company no longer exists, but it was then a prominent national developer and operator of many trophy properties. Many of the people who worked at Urban now hold positions in prominent real estate companies. Urban had a thorough methodology of how to pursue real estate development and investment that I carry with me today.

I also want to thank Bob Morgenstern at New York University, who incessantly encouraged me to write this book. Bob reviewed initial drafts of the manuscript and prepared some of the figures in the book. Similarly, I want to thank the many people at the New York University Real Estate Institute who allowed me to teach at the school and gave me the opportunity to refine much of the information I learned over my career.

I additionally want to thank my daughter, Victoria (Torie), who helped me with the editing of this book by highlighting areas that needed further explanation.

CHAPTER 1

Overview of the Development Process

Where does the real estate development process begin? It begins with an idea. It does not begin with crunching numbers. It does not necessarily begin with a site. It begins with an idea. Real estate development is a highly creative endeavor, as the reader will see. Frankly, those in the creative arts, such as movie or television production, often do very well transitioning into the real estate development industry.

ECONOMIC PERSPECTIVE

Before we delve too deeply into the development process, it is important to gain a perspective on its role in the U.S. economy. (Do not focus on the absolute numbers in the list below; instead, focus on the relative magnitude of the numbers as you read them.)

Real Estate Development[1]

- Is more than a US$5 trillion U.S. market segment
- Generates about a third of U.S. GDP
- Creates jobs for more than 9 million Americans
- Is responsible for nearly 70 percent of local property tax revenue, which pays for schools, roads, police, and other essential public services

Clearly, the real estate industry has a major impact on the U.S. economy, and on the world economy as well. I cannot think of any business or

---

[1]While these numbers are statistics from the United States, similar numbers and percentages proportionally exist for many other countries as well.

activity that does not directly or indirectly use real estate or is not a supplier of the real estate industry. Most important, focus on that last bullet point. If a municipality gets 70 percent of its revenue from property taxes, it is logical and true that municipalities are in favor of real estate development, that is, real estate development improves values and hence the tax base and thus generates increased property tax revenues. Therefore, municipalities inherently are positively inclined toward new property development and regeneration. Yes, there are municipalities that say they do not want new development, but eventually they all come around because property tax revenue has such a significant impact.

I mentioned earlier that the real estate industry has a major impact on the U.S. and world economy. Every business, every person, uses a building

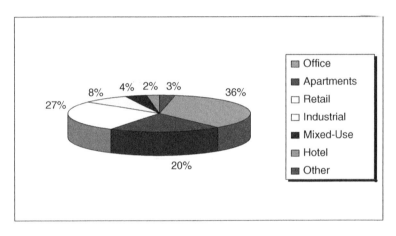

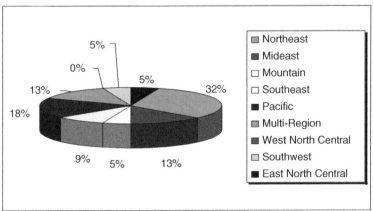

Figure 1.1a   200X REIT Transactions: Total Acquisitions US$9.7 Billion

or real estate every day. Even the homeless person sitting in a cardboard box has his piece of real estate. Hence, the balance sheet of every company and every person in this world has real estate as a major line item. Municipalities know this. Hence, over the years, governments have provided many financial and legal subsidies to enable additional real estate development and investment.

Let's look at Figures 1.1a and 1.1b.

Figures 1.1a and 1.1b were derived from information from public real estate investment trusts (REITs). The information is labeled as coming from 200X because the specific year is not important for this discussion. In Figure 1.1a, we see that REITs acquired US$9.7 billion of property. (The top pie charts indicate distribution of property types, and the bottom pie charts indicate geographic distribution.) In Figure 1.1b, we see that REITs

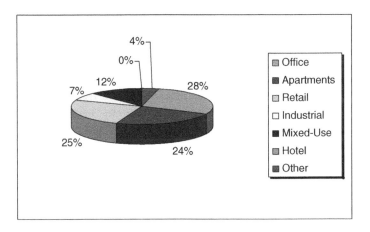

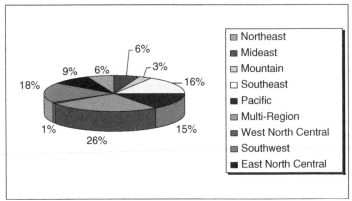

Figure 1.1b   200X REIT Transactions: Total Dispositions US$3.8 Billion

in this year disposed of or sold US\$3.8 billion of property. So, what do we learn by studying these pie charts? Well, we see that the REITs in this year are net holders of property. We see that the REITs concentrated their preferences in property type and concentrated their geography where the properties are located. So again, what do we learn from these pie charts? The correct answer is, as a developer, nothing; the information is useless. It is interesting but useless. Some might say that the information would be better presented as a trend over several years. Again, I would still say the information is useless to a developer. Primarily, when was this information gathered and presented? The data is from the end of a year. It probably took several weeks to compile the information into these nice pie charts. So, the information is outdated. A development project takes on average three to five years before construction begins, maybe another year or two for construction to finish, and perhaps another year before the building is fully occupied. So if a developer had a site today and started planning, before a building is completed and operating, five years or more will pass. What will the markets be like in five years? What will be the demands of any particular city or town five years from now? No one knows. So performing a trend analysis is barely a beginning. What a developer needs to do is establish the *trend beyond the trend*. Once a trend has been determined, the trend is old and common. A developer cannot gain an advantage by using known trend information. To be successful, a developer needs to perceive what is next to come. Now this is not easy to do, but this skill distinguishes successful developers from *very* successful developers.

Consider a group I worked with several years ago. The group presented an idea to me for creating a suite hotel project in New York City, seeking an opinion. The central idea was that the project would attract families. Currently, families had to secure multiple rooms to accommodate family members. A suite hotel would contain individual hotel rooms, but each room would contain two bedrooms, a sofa bed, and perhaps a folding cot. The group's concept included a children's museum on the ground floor, open to nonguests, and provided child care, should parents want to attend a Broadway show or go to dinner some evening. I thought this was a good idea. The next day, I received an e-mail newsletter that highlighted the fact that the concept was already being used in Germany. A week letter, I received another e-mail newsletter with an article discussing the concept in use in South Africa. Ideas, good ideas, are everywhere. Just because a developer has an idea rarely means he or she is the only person with that idea. There are many people in this world with good ideas. The key is to act quickly or to devise an idea that is the next step, or the trend beyond the trend.

A useful tip in trying to determine the trend beyond the trend is to look for the negative in a circumstance. That is, what is it that is not happening?

You will find that focusing on what is not happening is far easier than focusing on what is happening. Consider this example: Imagine you are with a friend, colleague, or spouse. There often comes a point when you might be a little hungry. So, what does one person say to the other? "I'm hungry. Where do you want to go to grab a bite?" What does the other person say? "I don't know. Where do you want to go?" And this questioning goes back and forth without immediate resolution. On the other hand, imagine if the dialogue went as follows: "I'm hungry. Where *don't* you want to go?" The answer usually comes quickly. "Well, I don't want Italian food because I just had Italian food last evening" (and so on). It is far easier to determine the negative because most people have definite ideas of the negative. A developer should do the same. Don't ask a city, "How about we build a shopping center here?" A developer should instead ask what the city does not want built. The answer often comes quickly.

Essentially, we are following demographic—that is, people—trends when we plan a real estate development. What are the population trends? What regional population or development shifts are occurring? Are there any specific city development trends discernible? In short, real estate development is about people. What is it that people are doing or, more important, not doing? If a developer becomes a student of people and how people go about their daily lives, that developer will become adept at formulating the trend beyond the trend.

The State of New Jersey created a number of years ago the Blueprint for Intelligent Growth (B.I.G.) Map. The color-coded map indicated where in the state the government would encourage development or regeneration, where in the state the government would discourage development or regeneration, and where in the state the government would be open to argument. These areas were depicted by the use of three colors: green, red, and yellow, respectively. (If you would like to look at the B.I.G. map, then go to the New Jersey Department of Environmental Protection web site.) To my knowledge, this is the only map of its kind created by any state in the country. It is a very creative and progressive effort for a state to exercise control on a statewide basis.

If you look closely at the B.I.G. Map, you will see a clear concentration of the green-colored areas. They are located across from the major cities of New York and Philadelphia. So why did New Jersey concentrate on these areas to encourage development? Well, what is physically in these areas? What is the condition of those improvements? The areas are built-up, but old. Infrastructure is inadequate and in need of repair. The state, in essence, has unproductive assets in these green areas. Unproductive assets from the government's viewpoint are assets that have low or nonexistent value for tax purposes. (Remember, 70 percent of property tax revenue supports the local municipality's efforts at maintaining roads, schools, and the like.) Therefore, it is easy to picture that where there is a concentration of non-productive assets, the government would like new development or regeneration. Conversely, the red-colored areas are already built, but the state would like to promote the preservation of open, green space and hence discourages additional development.

As I said, this is a creative and progressive effort. However, as of the writing of this book, the B.I.G. Map has been tabled indefinitely. That is, the purpose and execution of the B.I.G. Map will not be pursued for the foreseeable future. This is not to say that the concept was stopped. What happened? Well, what do you think would happen to elected officials in the red areas of the map? They would lose political power. How would this happen? Since new development would be discouraged in the red areas, the population would probably move to areas where they would find newer development (buildings). Thus the population in the red areas would probably decline. Along with reduced population and older buildings, property tax revenues would decline. With reduced property tax revenues, the town's basic and essential services would not be funded. Without the funding, politicians such as the mayor would initially be without purpose and eventually not have a town to govern.

In addition, New York and Pennsylvania were not too happy with the B.I.G. Map. The two states clearly understand that they would lose population to adjacent, newly rebuilt towns across the rivers in New Jersey, and as a result, the two states would lose tax revenue to New Jersey.

So, developers have to always address two factors when pursuing a development anywhere: What political changes will occur, and what property tax revenue changes will occur as a result of new development? Every town will ask this question, so be prepared with a logical answer.

RELEVANCY OF UNIVERSAL KNOWLEDGE

Everything you see, everything you hear, and everything you read is relevant to real estate development. Let me offer a couple of scenarios and take you through the thinking process of why universal knowledge is so important. Gasoline prices seem to be going higher, for a time they seemed to be going lower, but no one really knows what the trend is going to be. Recently, gasoline prices were at historically high prices, placing pressures on the population. What kind of pressures am I speaking about? Well, consider people who drive 30 minutes or more to get to their workplace or to a local train station to get to their workplace. When gasoline prices doubled or more, personal budgets were extended to pay for gasoline. These people who drive in many cases do not have a choice about driving because public commuter services are limited or nonexistent in the areas in which they live. Thus, they had to pay the higher gasoline prices. While many of these people were willing to bear the higher cost of gasoline, other expenses, particularly discretionary expenses, were reduced or eliminated. Perhaps people have become frustrated as a result of having to cut back on their luxuries or even their necessities of life as a result of the high gasoline prices. So what might be a commonsense solution? I suppose one possible solution might mean moving closer to the workplace or to the urban center. Very well; if people start moving closer to or into the city, what do they need? Where is the opportunity for a real estate developer? Well, the answer is quite simple. More housing has to be built in these urban centers.

One day you read in the newspaper that a foreign car manufacturer is moving into a southern U.S. state. What does that foreign car manufacturer need? Some argue that the foreign car manufacturer needs to move to a specific location that has a job pool of qualified employees for the manufacturing plant. Extending this thought, that means that perhaps new housing needs to be built to house the new employees. In addition to the new housing, perhaps some retail of various types has to be developed to service the people who are moving into the area. And of course, the foreign car manufacturer needs a building to establish the plant. Does this building exist currently? Does this building have to be built? On what site? If this building has to be built, what are the foreign car manufacturer's requirements? Again, another opportunity for a real estate developer.

Universal knowledge is critical. Always be aware of everything that is going on around you, whether you read about it in a newspaper, hear it on the radio, see it on television, or catch it on the Internet. This universal knowledge is an application of what I referred to earlier as the trend beyond the trend. If you, as a real estate developer, want to be successful, you will be aware of everything and be thinking about what opportunity is presenting itself to you.

> *"Don't forget nothing."*
> —Rogers' Standing Orders for Rangers, 1739

So, what is the development process? Let me offer a comprehensive, and somewhat lengthy, definition of the development process:

The improvement of raw land or property through the develop-
ment process is a highly creative process in which physical ingredi-
ents such as land and buildings are effectively combined with
financial and marketing resources to create an environment in
which people live, work, and play.

Let's dissect this definition, so you have a thorough understanding of
what the development process is really about.

The improvement of raw land or property. As a real estate developer,
you improve things, whether you are starting a development from
the ground up or renovating an existing property. When we say we
are improving raw land or property, what we really are saying is
that we are creating value. Many people who get involved with real
estate development think they want to get involved to make money.
The reality is that a real estate developer cannot make money without first creating value. Once value is created, then money or profit
can be made. This is a basic concept that I will refer to many times:
The main goal of a real estate developer is to create value.

A highly creative process. One characteristic that attracts many people to real estate development is that it is highly creative. In my
experience, some of the most successful people transitioning to real
estate development are those who come from the creative industries, such as film and television production and the like. Frankly, I
have learned that film and television production is actually very
similar in its processes to real estate development. The only thing
that's really different is the jargon. As a real estate developer, you
can do just about anything you wish to do. Of course, you have
limitations such as zoning, and you must meet all of the building
codes and other requirements. However, you can build or design
anything you wish. Your imagination and the imagination of your
project team are your limitations.

**Physical ingredients such as land and buildings are effectively com-
bined.** The fact that real estate development involves physicality
is very attractive to many people. People can actually see and
touch what it is that they do. They can point out to friends and
relatives a building that they themselves built. At one point in my
career, I was a commercial banker. When I was a real estate
banker, and I lent, say, US$100 million to a developer, I could see
how the US$100 million was used. I could touch a foundation,
touch a wall, or touch windows. Later in my career as a banker, I

lent to major corporations. I would lend, say, US$100 million to a Fortune 100 company. Where did that money go? Did it go to pay payroll? Was it used to pay administrative expenses? Could I touch something that the US$100 million was used to pay for? Most likely not. As a banker, I had a lot of confidence lending money to a developer because I knew I could see how the money was being spent. My consultants would tell me whether work was in place. When I was a corporate banker, I could only rely on auditors to tell me that the money was spent appropriately.

Financial and marketing resources. These two resources are essential to real estate developers. Clearly, financial resources are needed; otherwise, the developer would not have the money to build. But as this book explains, marketing and market research and the resources associated with the real estate development process are both essential.

Now, there are two things that I want everyone reading this book to adopt into their psyche. If there is nothing else that you learn by reading this book, there are two things that you must understand. The first is the last phrase in the definition of the development process: "to create an environment in which people live, work, and play." Some people new to the real estate development business still think that real estate is an anomaly. Some people think real estate is something that is highly specialized and doesn't involve the majority of people in the world. Well, think about it. Where are you now? Perhaps you are at home, at work, at school, in a park? All of these things involve real estate development. Perhaps they are buildings. Perhaps they are green space. All were created by a real estate developer. Everything that you do as a developer involves people and how they live, work, and play. When you go before a city board or a community group and they ask you, inevitably, "Why are you doing this development?" your answer should be immediate: "I am creating an environment by which people live, work, and play." If you say, as some inexperienced developers say, "I am here to make some money," you *will* fail to obtain the necessary approvals. Everyone knows that you would not, as a developer, be doing a development unless you made money. But you shouldn't be so crass as to say that's your sole purpose. The reality is that you are creating an environment by which people live, work, and play.

The second thing that is essential to your understanding of real estate development is the *enterprise concept*, as summarized by Jim Grasskamp of the University of Wisconsin at Madison. The enterprise concept portrays real estate development and its operations as a business, and it requires active, aggressive management. Consider, what is a business? A business has revenues, expenses, income, employees, and taxes. What does a real estate project have? A real estate project has revenues, expenses, income, employees, and taxes. They are essentially the same thing. What do both require to succeed and create value? They both require active and aggressive management. If you decide to passively monitor your business or real estate project, it will fail or, at the very least, be mediocre. So it is essential for a real estate developer to follow the enterprise concept.

Grasskamp said that you should perpetually ask yourself four questions:

1. **What is it that we are doing?**   What are you building? A hotel, a multifamily building, an office building, a retail complex? How big or small? How will it be designed? If real estate developers do not have a clear vision of what the market needs and what exactly they are building for the market, they will have difficulty.

2. **For whom are we doing it?**   Why is a real estate developer building a building? A developer doesn't build the building just for fun. A developer builds a building for a specific target market. Constantly ask yourself, For whom am I building this building? In reality, it doesn't matter what you think. What matters is what your target market thinks because it is your target market that is actually going to buy or lease space in your building.

3. **To whom are we doing it (whom are we affecting)?**   The reality is that a real estate developer who builds a building is causing change. That change could be increased traffic, noise, odors, or just the reality that something has changed. If a developer does not think about and identify those groups or individuals who will be affected by the real estate development, those groups or individuals will become that developer's NIMBYs (Not in My Backyard people).

4. **Will it economically fly?**   Is your project financially feasible? Note that the financial analysis is the fourth thing that Grasskamp asked about, not the first thing, as many people think. While it's true that financial feasibility is important, as far as a real estate development project is concerned, it is clearly not the first consideration and can be irrelevant if the first three questions are not sufficiently answered.

If real estate developers do not know what they are doing, if real estate developers do not know for whom they are building, if real estate developers do not know whom their project is affecting, then the financial feasibility is absolutely useless information. I have interacted with a number of real estate developers who have proudly announced that their project has a projected return on investment of 50 percent or more but really did not understand the ideal or desired project they should be building for their target market or how the surrounding community and government would be affected by their new real estate development. Unfortunately, in many cases, developers do not ask themselves these four questions. They do not apply the enterprise concept, and as a result, they have mediocre projects. Oftentimes, they wonder why their project is not leasing or selling. The answer is simple: They did not apply the enterprise concept.

Grasskamp goes on to talk about the highest and best use versus the most fitting use and the highest and best use versus the most fitting use versus the most probable use. What does this mean? Let me offer a hypothetical situation. Let's say that you have acquired a strip of land between a light industrial area and a residential single-family home area. The concept of highest and best use would argue that you should build another industrial plant—a property type that likely creates the highest value for the site in this situation. Do you think the single-family homeowners would appreciate having an industrial plant in their backyard? If you built single-family homes on the strip of land, would anybody buy these homes next to an industrial plant? You could build a retail building. Single-family homeowners would probably appreciate having retail and similar services close by. But would the single-family homeowners appreciate the delivery trucks coming and going at 6:30 in the morning? So what should be built? Try to answer the first three questions that Grasskamp says you should be asking yourself in this hypothetical.

Grasskamp further said that there are three types of development approaches or concepts: the traditional development concept, the idealistic development concept, and the pragmatic development concept.

The traditional development concept is quite successfully used every day by many people. Under the traditional development concept, a developer finds a site, comes up with an idea, pulls together a team, signs contracts, builds the building, leases it, and sells it. Again, the traditional development concept is used every day by many developers, and there is absolutely nothing wrong with the approach.

The idealistic development concept is perhaps what you the reader will be using. The idealistic approach suggests optimization of consumer satisfaction. That is, you know the target market's needs and wants, and you, as a developer, try to maximize the satisfaction of your target market's needs and wants. Next, you try to minimize your cost of production, you try to minimize the impact on third parties (NIMBYs), and last, you try to maximize the profit to the investors (including your profit).

But Grasskamp said that a developer is likely to use the pragmatic development concept. The pragmatic development concept says that a real estate development results in having less than the most fitting use, which is constrained by political factors, short-term solvency, and the state of real estate technology. Let's look at each one of these individual aspects of the definition of pragmatic development concept. Let's consider these point by point:

Less than most fitting use. It often arises when a site is available but cannot have the maximum highest and best use because of the needs and wants of the surrounding neighbors, as in the hypothetical of a strip of land between a light industrial park and a single-family housing development.

Constrained by political factors. What is one of the most common political factors that constrains real estate? It is zoning. Zoning requires a developer to include certain aspects and elements into his future project. There are many other political constraints, such as political elections, but zoning is the most common.

Short-term solvency. Short-term solvency is probably the most important aspect of development. Short-term solvency asks whether you have the money to bring the development project to fruition, where fruition is defined as the point at which you are able to get a construction loan for your project. For example, do you have the money to pay for attorneys, accountants, soil-testing consultants, environmental testing consultants, and so on? Short-term solvency is very much like the old adage about investing in the stock market, spend only the money that you can afford to lose. Until you reach the point that you actually are able to get a construction loan for your project, all the money that you spend will come out of your own personal savings account. Perhaps you will be able to raise money from friends and family, but it is still money that comes from your own savings or out of your own pocket. There is no standard for how much a developer will spend on a proposed project to bring it to the point of obtaining a construction loan. It could be a small amount because the developer has a lot of experience in building a particular type of property in a particular location. It could be a large amount because of various difficulties or the sheer scale of the project. I mentioned that the time to bring a project to the point of obtaining a construction loan could be 2 to 3 years or could be 10, 15, 20, or 30 years. A rough, rough rule of thumb I often use is that the predevelopment costs (the amount of money that will be spent before a construction loan is obtained) is about 3 percent of the eventual total development cost for the project. With that in mind, I often use the amount of US$200,000 to US$300,000 given the size of projects I have worked on. (The amount could be lower or significantly higher.) Short-term solvency asks whether you as the developer have US$200,000 to US$300,000 readily available to spend on the predevelopment costs of a proposed project, money that you can afford to lose and not have a significant change in your lifestyle if you cannot bring the project to fruition. Many beginning developers have a simple answer to this question: no. So a developer who thought of building a US$30 million office building in the suburbs somewhere is often forced to revise the plan to renovating a two-story walk-up building in the city.

The state of real estate technology.   This is not about technology as in computers. I am addressing building technology, design technology, and the like. With all due respect to design architects, they often design a building that cannot be built. Thus the question here is what technology will allow the efficient and cost-effective construction of a building that is attractively designed by your design architects?

All of this is the concept of pragmatic development. Pragmatic development is more than likely the approach that you and everyone else will use toward the development of a new project.

I like Figure 1.2 because of its simplicity, yet the simplicity quite effectively shows how a developer brings together a variety of resources to create

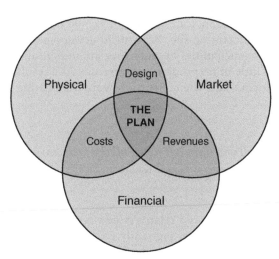

Figure 1.2   The Development Process

a development plan. For example, when a developer takes the universe of physical things and combines it with the universe of the market, the developer has the design of the project. When the developer takes the universe of physical things and combines it with the financial tools, the developer has the costs of the project. When the developer takes market information and resources and combines it with the financial resources, the developer has the revenues for the project. When all three things are combined—physical, market, financial—then the developer has created the development plan.

GROUND-UP DEVELOPMENT VERSUS REDEVELOPMENT

There are three basic types of development: greenfield development, brownfield development, and grayfield development.

Greenfield development takes place on a site where nothing has ever been built previously. The sites may be old farmland or forest areas. Greenfield development once was the most common type of development, as suburbanization continued out from the central business districts (CBDs). Today, greenfield development is probably the most difficult type of property development to execute.

Brownfield development has two definitions. The first, or technical, definition is a site that has environmental contamination. The common or day-to-day definition of brownfield development is basically a site that has been built on before. The site could be improved with a structure or structures or the site could be vacant. So, for example, this could be an abandoned industrial plant or manufacturing site. Brownfield development sites are of high interest to most municipalities because they are nonproductive assets; that is, they produce little or no property tax revenue. As a result, municipalities welcome developers and their efforts toward renovating or reclaiming brownfield sites.

> *"Education is all you have left when all the facts are gone."*
> —Brigadier General Daniel Kaufman, Dean, U.S. Military Academy

Grayfield development is a relatively new term that is being used more frequently today. There is nothing really wrong with a grayfield site. It is often improved with a building, the building is fully leased, and the property is cash flowing; that is, there is sufficient cash flow for the property to pay all of its expenses, taxes, and the like. What distinguishes a grayfield property is that it is in need of renovation or is currently being physically underutilized. So, for example, let's say we have a 10,000-square-foot convenience center. The convenience center is fully leased with the typical tenants of a dry cleaner, video store, take-out food, and so on and pays all of its expenses and taxes. However, the 10,000-square-foot convenience center is located on 100 acres of land. Clearly, the property is being underutilized. The property could be greatly expanded to create higher value through highest and best use. Most developers acquire grayfield properties. Without question, all beginning developers should focus all of their efforts toward acquiring grayfield properties. Why?

It is not unusual that a new developer who acquires a grayfield property begins a redevelopment effort. Somewhere during the process, the new developer perhaps feels overwhelmed, perhaps thinks that he or she has gotten involved in something that is beyond his or her capabilities. Frustrated and frightened, the new developer decides to sell the grayfield property. Can a sale be made? Absolutely. The property is cash flowing, has value, and can be readily sold to another party. Let's say the new developer decides to help his community by purchasing a brownfield property. Again, somewhere in the process, the new developer feels overwhelmed. Can the developer sell the brownfield site? Sure. But when? How much is the property worth? The biggest distinction between a brownfield development site and a grayfield development site is that the grayfield development site has cash flow.

THE SIX PHASES OF DEVELOPMENT

Throughout the development process, you will be involved in a variety of development activities:

Site acquisition	Cost planning and control
Market/program planning	Financial
Leasing	Project timing and scheduling
Property management/operations	Community approval/zoning
Architecture/engineering/construction	Documentation
	And so on

To keep yourself organized and on track, you need a plan. That plan is the six phases to the development process:

1. Study phase
2. Feasibility phase

3. Preconstruction phase
4. Construction phase
5. Initial occupancy phase
6. Occupancy and investment management phase

Simplistically, in the study phase, you do some basic analysis and investigation, perhaps focusing on a city, neighborhood, or even a site or two. Once you are reasonably confident about a particular site, you proceed into the feasibility phase, in which your goal is a feasibility report. (A feasibility report is a business plan for a project, as discussed at length in a later chapter.) See Figures 1.3a through 1.3d. After completing your feasibility study and deciding to move forward, you enter the preconstruction phase. In this phase, you are preparing for physical construction. You will be acquiring the site, obtaining government approvals, and signing contracts for the physical construction of the project. The construction phase is the construction of your project, including construction management. The initial occupancy phase includes the move-in of tenants and tenant improvement work. The last phase, the occupancy and investment management phase, includes the move-in of the remaining tenants and the continuous analysis and management of the newly built or renovated building through and including the

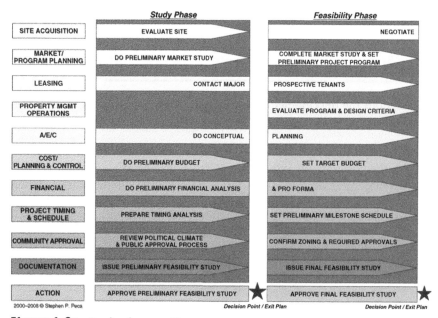

Figure 1.3a Predevelopment Process

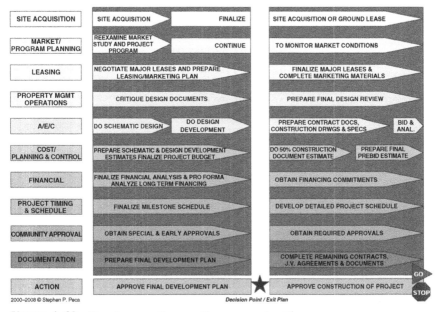

Figure 1.3b Development Process: Preconstruction Phase

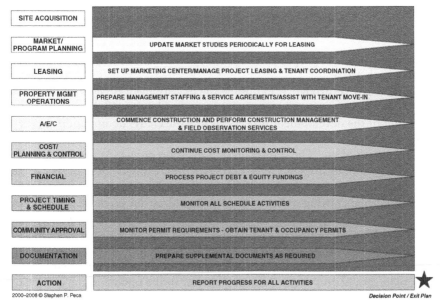

Figure 1.3c Development Process: Construction Phase and Initial Occupancy Phase

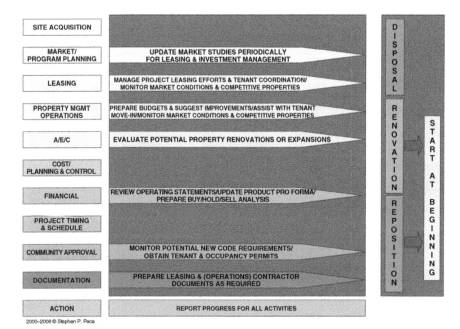

Figure 1.3d Development Process: Occupancy and Investment Management Phase

eventual sale of the property. The remainder of the book speaks to the details in each phase.

Figures 1.3a through 1.3d outline the development process graphically. They show the various activities that a developer will be involved in throughout the development process. While the charts do not address every activity, they address the major and most common activities. Notice the star between each phase. The stars represent decision points. At the end of each phase, you should stop and reflect on your progress and consciously decide whether to move forward into the next phase. Of course, this means that you should be crafting an exit plan for each decision point. The exit plan asks, How do I stop the process? How do I recover my costs to date? What can I do? Many developers I know—even large developers—have exit plans, but interestingly, these developers have exit plans only after the occupancy phase. That is, their exit plan is to sell the project. Brilliant! But what is your exit plan should you need to exit the project in the middle of the construction phase? What do you do? Many developers have not thought about this situation. You *must* have an exit plan for each phase in the development process. When thinking about each exit plan—and for that matter, as you progress through each phase—you should ask yourself, Have I created value? If you have created value, you have something to sell; this is the ideal. As a corollary, do not spend any money unless you can say to yourself, If I spend this money, I will be creating value. For example, to spend money on a market analysis report in the study phase does not typically create value. At this phase, your idea is probably not fully thought out. Hence, the market analysis report would be generic, not useful to anyone else, and thus of no or very little value to anyone else. On the other hand, if you obtain a phase 1 environmental assessment on a particular site, you will know at the conclusion of the assessment whether the particular site has environment contamination. This knowledge clearly establishes value (or detracts from it) for that particular site.

The charts outlined in Figures 1.3a through 1.3d are clear, comprehensive, and simple to understand. However, there is one reality that the charts do not recognize: The development process will never happen this way. The development process will occur in an apparently haphazard way, totally different from what is outlined on the chart. Still, you must perform all of the activities outlined on the chart; otherwise, your development process or plan will be incomplete and thus either fail, be fraught with numerous problems, or be mediocre at best.

Let me offer an example of why the development process will never occur as outlined. Let's say you are offered a prime piece of property. From existing knowledge, you know the property is fully occupied, cash flowing, and in good physical shape. It is being offered to you at a substantial discount. Most people in the real estate industry acknowledge that if the sales price of a property is less than the replacement cost of the property, you should buy the property. This means that you will have acquired the property well before the study phase begins instead of sometime during the feasibility phase, as outlined on the chart. This situation is not an unusual circumstance. However, after acquiring the property, you must perform all of the activities outlined; otherwise, you will suffer endless problems and perhaps fail in your efforts. The development process includes many functional activities; *all* must be performed.

So given what we have discussed in this chapter, what is the role of a developer? The developer is a visionary. The developer is a manager and coordinator of people. Accordingly, the developer is a team builder who persuades the team to embrace her or his vision and leadership toward the ultimate goal of the creation of a building and the creation of value. The developer is a problem solver. I would say that the majority of a developer's time will be spent on solving a variety of minor and major problems. Many of these problems can be anticipated. Many of these problems occur without notice or unexpectedly. A developer is also a public spokesperson who will need to constantly talk about the project and sell the need for the project to each of the constituencies.

So, is a specific education or specific knowledge needed to be a developer? No, not really. Anyone can be a developer, but anyone can fail as a developer, too. I think there are three areas that a developer should be comfortable with to be successful. The first is accounting and finance. You do not have to be an accountant or a CPA. You should just be comfortable with numbers, since you will be faced with them every day. The second is knowledge of the law, specifically contract law. Everything you do in development involves a contract, so you should be comfortable reading and interpreting contracts. The third is public speaking and/or public relations. You will be making many, many presentations to groups of people and sometimes to just a single person. You should be comfortable making these presentations and dealing with people who disagree or heckle you.

LEARNING POINTS FROM THIS CHAPTER

After reading this chapter, I should:

- Understand the distinction between construction and development.
- Know the definition of *development* and specifically three words that always define development.
- Understand the enterprise concept.
- Know the six phases of development and the importance of an exit plan at the end of each phase.

CHAPTER 2

Business Ethics

This chapter talks about the complexity and importance of business ethics in real estate development. The two sections of this chapter address the relevance of ethics to the real estate industry and legislated ethics.

RELEVANCY TO THE REAL ESTATE INDUSTRY

The real estate industry is a very close-knit business. As a result, it seems that everyone knows everyone. I am sure that you have heard from popular culture the phrase "six degrees of separation." In the real estate development business, I think there are really only two degrees of separation. No matter what you do in the real estate business, it is very easy for anyone to learn about your activities. I can easily find out what anyone's done in the business, and anyone can find out the same about me. What is really important is a person's integrity. I have heard stories of developers who have promoted poor quality control on buildings on one coast of a country. By poor quality control, I mean poor workmanship, aggressive business techniques, shoddy materials, and the like. So, the developer finishing his building on one coast of a country thinks he can avoid his mistakes by pursuing a project on the opposite coast. What do you think that planning departments in cities on the opposite coast will do first as they consider this developer's proposal? Of course, they check into the references of that new developer and, of course, find out about the poor workmanship, aggressive business techniques, shoddy materials, and the like.

Several years ago, I needed to speak with a large developer in Russia. It literally took only one telephone call to find out the name of this developer in Russia. Two degrees of separation—never forget this rule. Just as much as I am encouraging you to research the people that you are doing business with, those same people are researching you. Your personal integrity is paramount in the real estate business. Your integrity, as perceived by your peers, will govern and direct the type and amount of business that you're going to do in the real estate development industry.

> *"Real estate used to be a hedge against inflation. Now it's a hedge against disaster. You won't lose your money. In a worst-case scenario, instead of a 9 percent yield, you get a 6 percent yield."*
> —Cooper Stuart, head of the capital markets desk at Ernst & Young, in
> *Dallas Business Journal*, August 18, 2003

What we're really speaking about is ethics in an environment of change. These changes consist of the following:

- Economic changes
- Societal changes
- Technological changes

One of the biggest economic changes in this country is moving from industrial businesses to service businesses. While we can argue which is better or which is worse, the reality is that the change causes new markets and opportunities and, as a result of these new markets and opportunities, new demands from the consuming public. In short, the needs of the population have changed. We have seen a tremendous amount of acceleration in how business and industry in the United States has changed over even just the last 10 years. If you can imagine the amount of change that has occurred in the last 50 years, the amount of change is mind-boggling.

Society is clearly changing. Demographic changes mean more diversity (more than ever before in the history of the United States). Societal changes and requirements result from new cultures, and these new cultures bring new desires and needs to the existing society. Some of these desires and needs have never been seen or experienced before by Americans—let alone other countries. All countries have similar issues and concerns regarding, for example, immigration into their countries. It seems in all circumstances, the consuming public is asking for more convenience—no, not really asking for more convenience, demanding more convenience. A perfect example of this convenience, which is even being now asked of their employers, is being able to work at home. The consuming public is constantly on the go, whether that means people, families, or individuals.

One of the biggest changes that has occurred in the last 10 years or so has been the Internet. The Internet, I argue, is actually one of the best and worst things that has happened to real estate developers. Given this chapter's subject, the Internet has caused more stress and anxiety than any other type of technology. Think about it: Information flows almost instantaneously. If you as a developer want to keep up on the most current information in your locale, in your city, or in your country—or another country, for that matter—you have to be constantly surfing the Internet. What's worse is that the consuming public expects that you are surfing the Internet and have the most current information. If you do not, you lose your competitive advantage. So what do these changes mean to us? Well, we all now have more stress and pressure. As I mentioned before, we have to keep up with new information as it becomes available. If you don't keep up with the information, again, you lose your competitive advantage. And as you get this information, it's imperative that you transmit this information, perhaps with some sort of analysis, to your clients as quickly as possible.

Let's step back for a moment and define some terms. I do not intend this chapter to provide you with an entire course in business ethics, but you should understand some basic terms. One such term is *principles*. Principles are moral guidelines, rules, and obligations. Probably the most common principle that we all know is the Golden Rule: Do unto others as you would have them do unto you. A second term to understand is values. Values are temporary. They could be moral or immoral. They could be legal or illegal. What I'm really trying to explain here is that ethics is equal to actions. Ethics is really about what you do or don't do.

Why are ethics more of an issue in real estate? Real estate, again, is a very close and networked global community. Reputations matter more. Remember what I mentioned earlier about two degrees of separation? I cannot stress this concept enough. Two major aspects of the real estate environment cause ethical issues. First, many problems arise from the low barrier to entry into the industry. Second, the real estate industry is generally unregulated. One doesn't need a license to be a real estate developer. Yes, you need a license to be an architect, a broker, or a contractor, but to be a developer, you simply need to have an idea and, most important, have the money. Hence the real estate development industry and developers in general have a negative reputation from past developers who did not follow ethical practices.

More specifically, what is it about the business that causes ethical issues in real estate? Frankly, by its nature, real estate development is an environment that causes many, many issues: the pressure to meet investment goals, huge cash outlays, the low barriers to entry, new markets and opportunities, and so on.

LEGISLATED ETHICS

I would be very surprised if you've never heard of the Sarbanes-Oxley Act of 2002 and the PATRIOT Act. However, you may not be aware of what they mean and how they affect you as the real estate developer.

Sarbanes-Oxley was supposedly the fastest legislation ever passed by the U.S. Congress. The legislation was meant to address the problems caused by companies such as WorldCom and Enron. The act requires that all public U.S. companies pay more diligence to their business activities and systems of internal controls. The act is not solely focused toward financial reporting but also includes general business operations, such as how the business markets its products, its quality control, and how it hires, fires, and trains its personnel. The act pierces the corporate veil. Previously, the chief financial officer or controller of a public corporation signed the various SEC documents. Now, the president and chief operating officer and/or chairman must also sign the SEC documents. Each is now *personally* responsible for the information contained in the SEC filing documents. Let's say you've been incredibly successful and are now president of a major multinational corporation. Your company has operations in almost every country of the world. How comfortable do you feel about signing SEC documents that incorporate your operations in a remote country where the language and culture, let alone business operating practices, differ dramatically from your own? How comfortable do you feel about placing your residence, car, and personal finances at risk? Well, you are probably thinking I am off-topic. I said that Sarbanes-Oxley was only applicable to public corporations. You are a real estate developer. You have absolutely no intention of being a public company. You plan to go into business by yourself or with one or two business partners.

Did you possibly consider doing business with a REIT? Many REITs are public corporations. So, if you do business with a public REIT, you will have to comply with the Sarbanes-Oxley Act. All right, you have absolutely no intention of doing business with a public REIT. Will you possibly do business with a contractor, architect, or broker who is a public corporation? Again, you will have to comply with the Sarbanes-Oxley Act.

Very well, you plan to establish the policy of doing business with only private companies who have no Sarbanes-Oxley Act requirements. The Sarbanes-Oxley Act has been around for a few years now. While most of the general public does not know the details of the act, the public understands the intentions of the act. I know of several circumstances where developers who are trying to raise money from investors have had difficulty.

Consider that you have you created a comprehensive feasibility study for a US$100 million mixed-use project. You have just met with a group of investors interested in your project. Your presentation to the investors was extremely successful. The investors are excited about your project. They are ready to write a check for your equity requirements. But one of the investors has a question: "I am sure you are familiar with the Sarbanes-Oxley Act and all of the reporting requirements. I completely realize that you are a private company. I don't expect you to have all the systems and controls required of the act. However, I wonder, what sorts of internal controls do you have in your business?" The typical reaction you might have is a blank stare. You are not a big company, let alone a public company. You have no idea how to answer the investor's question. Your silence and mystified facial expression cause the investors to make the assumption that you have no internal controls and systems. The investors are forced to conclude that they do not feel comfortable investing a huge sum of money into your project.

The investor's question should not catch you by surprise. All the investor wants to hear is that you have basic controls and systems. The investor wants to hear that you use an accounting system. The investor wants to hear that you require dual signatures on checks. The investor wants to hear that you do something!

The PATRIOT Act, among other things, requires that when a person raises money (takes deposits, makes investments for another, etc.), the person knows where the money comes from. Did the money come from an illegal source? Is the money coming from illegal activities? Does the money come from somebody on the U.S. government's watch list? The PATRIOT Act makes it the responsibility of the person—in our case, the developer—to know the source of money invested in his or her project.

So, how do you take ethical actions? It starts with a logical progression of decision making, that is:

- Identify the problem.
- List the facts.
- Identify the characters.
- Review the alternatives.
- Reflect on whom the decision will affect.

The points are typical of how anyone would analyze a case study. That is to say, none of these points are profound. All that anyone can ask is that you consider a methodology when making a decision and that you are logical in making your decision. Frankly, no one can really criticize you for making a dumb decision as long as you are logical in identifying the problem, listing the facts, identifying the characters, reviewing the alternatives, and reflecting on whom the decisions will affect.

So, good ethics is about good risk management. As I pursue the development business, there are some general rules of thumb I like to follow.

Be transparent. I like to follow the policy of transparency when doing business with anyone. It is very difficult for anyone to find fault when they have had all the information they needed up front. In my experience, transparency will always help you succeed whenever questions are raised about your actions. I often use a metaphor to explain the concept of transparency. You have an investor. You give the investor an offering memorandum or a thorough, comprehensive feasibility study. I like to metaphorically take a pickup truck, fill the back of the pickup truck with all the papers associated with my project, drive to the investor's house, and dump all the paper on the investor's front lawn. Then, later, when the investor comes to me and says, "You never told me about this!" I can confidently tell the investor that he has had all the information associated with the investment. It is his fault that he didn't read through the material. Transparency, I find, seems to solve many problems.

Another concept that helps in the promulgation of good ethics is to seek experience and to know what you don't know. I suppose you could paraphrase this sentence and generally call the concept humility. I have been in the real estate business for quite some time, yet I don't know everything (and yet I have written this book). I am willing to acknowledge that I don't know everything. If I did, why would I have to put together a specialist project team to accomplish a development? As a corollary to knowing what you don't know, always question the assumptions you or others make. I often take the stance of asking dumb questions like "Could you show me how to do this or how you calculated that number?" I find that often I learn more information about other people and their work than I could ever learn by just reading through the papers or analyzing numbers. Ask questions. Always keep reminding yourself that you are ultimately responsible for the actions you take. If you rely on someone else's assumptions without having asked questions about those assumptions, and those assumptions are wrong, then you are taking on more risk than you really should.

In all of this, be sure to communicate. Communication is essential for anybody doing business. Risks should be discussed openly. The number one reason cited by many for why management or project teams fail is lack of or poor communication. You have complete control over how much or how little communication you have with your project team. The level of communication that you have, coupled with transparency, will determine the amount of success you have in your development project. Frankly, I am not upset by problems because I know that problems occur constantly in real estate development. However, I want someone to communicate these problems to me so I can resolve them. If the problems are not communicated to me, then I become upset.

One of the most difficult things in real estate development is constant change. So a good developer, in order to manage constant change, will show constant discipline. The rule of thumb here is to convert routine activities into habit. Developers will always have problems. I can guarantee you that as a real estate developer, you will face problems. I cannot tell you what those problems will be or what the magnitude of those problems will be, only that you will have problems. So, if you convert mundane things into habits so that you do not have to worry about them or worry about your project team worrying about them, you can focus your talents where they should be focused—on solving the problems.

> *"The hotel industry isn't overbuilt, it's under-demolished."*
> —Lou Plasencia, president and CEO of the Plasencia Group,
> GlobeSt.com, August 7, 2003

A real estate developer also needs to use common sense. If something doesn't seem right, if something seems too good to be true, then you should trust your intuition, your common sense. Of all the various developers and, for that matter, investors that I've dealt with, common sense seems to be one of the characteristics most lacking in these people.

Always remember that return is only half of the equation. There have been numerous times when I have had a junior analyst working for me with the basic fault of focusing on return and not using common sense. For example, the junior analyst gets a deal book from a broker about a project. The junior analyst runs off, tears open the information package, and begins to do extensive financial analysis on the project. Two or three days later, the junior analyst comes to me and says we must do this project. He claims that the return that we could earn on our investment is substantial. I listen to the junior analyst and then ask a very simple question: "Have you seen the project?" Almost always, the response is no. So I ask the junior analyst to get in his car, grab a taxi, or catch a flight and visit the project site. In most cases, I receive a phone call from the junior analyst, who sheepishly tells me that the project should not be pursued. He then goes on to tell me, for example, that the project site is located between a waste treatment plant and a junkyard and that, as a result, it would be impossible to successfully build and sell high-end condominium residences on the site. The moral of the story, I explain to the junior analyst, is that he should never have wasted his time crunching numbers without having seen the site. Seeing a site and using common sense would have quickly lead to the investment decision being negative. Instead, the junior analyst wasted two or three days doing a financial analysis. Return is only half the equation.

LEARNING POINTS FROM THIS CHAPTER

After reading this chapter, I should:

- Understand why ethics are important in the real estate industry, more so than in any other industry.
- Understand how to attempt to make ethical decisions.
- Understand that certain laws exist that legislate ethics and your responsibilities under the law.
- Understand that the practice of ethical behavior is directly related to risk management.

CHAPTER 3

Project and Development Teams

This chapter discusses the importance of the project and development teams needed for any real estate development. No development can be successfully completed without the proper selection of team members and the formation of a team.

TYPES OF DEVELOPERS

There are different types of developers that you will encounter in the real estate development business. To clarify the general types of developers, I have broken them down into three broad developer types and their business objectives:

1. Private-sector developer
2. Not-for-profit developer
3. Public-sector developer

The private-sector developer is perhaps what you will be as you embark upon your real estate development business. While working on your development project, you charge and earn a developer's fee that is typically based on the total development costs of your project. In addition to your development fee, you will earn a reversionary profit on the sale of that project. The development fee that you earn is essentially to pay for your administrative costs, food, and living expenses during development, because during development there is no cash flow from the project. The bulk of the money that you will earn will come from your reversionary profit on the sale of that project.

> *"Teamwork is the ability to work together toward a common vision. The ability to direct individual accomplishments toward organizational objectives. It is the fuel that allows common people to attain uncommon results."*
>
> —Andrew Carnegie

Not-for-profit developers primarily earn their money from the developer's fee, which is higher than the private-sector developer's fee. The reason for this is simple. Not-for-profit developers will not have a principal interest (ownership) in the projects they work on. They are not entitled to any reversionary profit from the sale of projects. Thus, the incentive for not-for-profit developers is the developer's fee—which has positive and negative aspects. The private-sector developer potentially has huge financial rewards after completion of a project; accordingly, the private-sector developer takes a tremendous amount of risk to obtain that reward. Conversely, there are no guarantees that a private-sector developer will obtain any money.

The not-for-profit developer has the advantage of working in a niche market of primarily privately owned hospitals and schools. However, these not-for-profit entities fund themselves through annual allocations. Thus, if the not-for-profit client runs out of money in a given fiscal year, the not-for-profit developer may not get paid the developer's fee until the next fiscal period.

Public-sector developers are similar to not-for-profit developers in that they only earn a developer's fee and are not entitled to a reversionary profit, as private-sector developers are. Also like the not-for-profit developers, the public-sector developers operate in a niche market building hospitals, schools, and buildings for governments. The construction of these buildings is highly specialized, and the project volume is low. So a public-sector developer can do quite well. In addition, the public-sector developer has a rated government as a client and will get paid.

FUNCTIONAL DISCIPLINES IN THE DEVELOPMENT PROCESS

The real estate development process uses a multitude of functional activities, as shown in the development process chart in Chapter 1.

- Legal
- Environmental
- Marketing
- Finance

- Architecture
- Engineering
- Construction
- Quality control
- Management
- And so on

A developer will utilize all of these functions. The questions is whether you as a developer can do all of these things. Can you do some of them? As we discussed in Chapter 1, there is no specific knowledge or education needed by a developer to be successful. Even if you have the skill to perform all of these functions, you are only one person, and there are still only 24 hours in the day. So a developer needs consultants and needs to organize a project or development team.

> *"The best executive is the one who has sense enough to pick good men to do what he wants done, and self-restraint enough to keep from meddling with them while they do it."*
> —Theodore Roosevelt

These team members or consultants (I am using the word *consultants* in a very general way to include contractors, attorneys, and the like) are hired by the developer to work on a specific project. Some developers have these functions in-house, but as a beginning developer, you certainly do not have the proceeds or, for that matter, the business volume to justify hiring a number of employees. But consider that once a developer brings these functions in-house, the developer's cost basis drops dramatically. For example, if you as a developer are working on three projects, you will probably hire an architect for each project and probably a different architect for each of the projects. You will pay the full amount of the architects' fees. On the other hand, if you hire an architect as an employee, the architect gets paid a salary whether working on three or a hundred projects, and so the developer's cost per project for an architect drops dramatically. Extend and multiply these savings to attorneys, accountants, marketing, and on down the list, and you can see the benefit of having a development firm.

But when you use employees on projects, your employees must be aware of and maintain a semblance of independence. As a simple example, if you have staff appraisers in your firm, you cannot use an appraisal report written by one of your staff appraisers to submit to a bank for bank financing. There is a lack of independence and impartiality.

> *"Command is a matter of wisdom, integrity, humanity, courage, and discipline."*
>
> —Sun Tzu, sixth century B.C.

The following is a broad list of consultants typically employed on development projects:

Market analyst	Determines usability of site, size, market niches, timing
Architect	Designs buildings
Engineer	Designs utilities, roads, sewer, water
Land planner	Handles layout of building and parking
Landscape architect	Plans and selects plants, trees, shrubs, vegetation
Contractors	Both general contractors and subcontractors build structures and do site preparation
Environmental consultant	Checks for prior contamination and wetlands, flood plains, other problems
Transportation consultants	Size internal and external streets, and traffic signals
Appraiser	Values property for loan purposes
Attorneys	Writes contracts, handles title work as needed, and may help with legal structuring
Accountants	Deal with tax issues, keep development books, and may help with budgeting and financial structuring
Real estate brokers	Sell property for a commission
Leasing agents	Lease space to commercial tenants, also for a commission
Marketing and public relations	Make sure space is occupied and sales among commercial tenants are as high as possible
Property managers	Manages day-to-day problems, collects rents, and improves property value

Once again, this is a broad and basic list. It is likely you will not use everyone on this list.

It is important to demand that your consultants not limit their work to simply providing you with a summary of the current circumstances. Your consultants should also provide specific, realistic, and tangible solutions to any issues or problems uncovered during their work. This is important. You will be paying each consultant handsomely. You must never forget the concept of short-term solvency. Make sure each consultant provides you with usable and practical solutions.

Thus, you should organize your development team by focusing on your need, the timing, and their cost. Only use a consultant when you need a consultant. I often have seen beginning developers start the development process by hiring an attorney. The beginning developer understands that everything done in development involves legal matters, so who better to help the beginning developer, right? An attorney (1) may not have the specialized experience and (2) may bill services at multiple hundreds of dollars per hour. You must never forget the concept of short-term solvency. Many beginning developers go financially bankrupt using this approach. Also, how should your consultant be paid? By the hour? A flat fee? Sweat equity? A rule of thumb I often use is to ask myself, If I spend money, will that money spent increase the value of the project? If by spending the money, project value increases, then yes, I should spend the money. If by spending the money, value does not change, then I should wait until the time when spending the money increases value. Say I decide to hire a market analyst to research a market. Does this research report increase the project's value? It might increase my knowledge, but that is an intangible investment. Let's say I have located a property and placed it under contract to perform due diligence for a possible acquisition. If I spend money on a phase 1 environmental study, I will learn whether the property has or does not have contamination. That knowledge will definitely affect the value of the property, so it is appropriate to spend the money at this time.

Sweat equity from a consultant is an important tool for every developer. This means that a consultant provides services in hopes of obtaining a contract for work with the developer. The developer often pays nothing for the services at this stage. As far as the consultant is concerned, these unpaid services are a cost of marketing. As far as the developer is concerned, the developer is getting useful information or services for free. You must never forget the concept of short-term solvency. For example, when would you engage a property manager? Many inexperienced developers might say you should engage a property manager when the building is about to be opened for tenants. Wrong! Property managers should be contacted during the design phase of the project. (Note that I used the word contacted and not engaged or hired in this sentence.) The property manager can comment on layout, material selections, and other matters that will have an impact on the future operating costs of the project. This information is incredibly valuable to a developer because lowering the operating cost of a building before it is built means that the value of the building will be increased when the building is built and operational. Does a developer pay for this advice? Perhaps, but generally no. The property manager is hoping to show off his or her expertise with the goal of being contractually hired and perhaps is investing sweat equity.

All that said, you should do as much of the work yourself as you can. Maybe you are a trained architect, attorney, engineer, or accountant. Then use your knowledge and skill to do the work, and do not hire a consultant. You must never forget the concept of short-term solvency.

FACTORS TO CONSIDER WHEN FORMING A DEVELOPMENT TEAM

Choose your consultants and form your team wisely. There are three key factors for choosing members of your development team:

1. Skill and aptitude
2. Experience
3. Compatibility

Frankly, all the consultants have the skill and aptitude to do their work. So you should focus on their experience—not overall experience, but *experience with the type of project you are planning where you are building it*. You can hire, say, an architect who specializes in office buildings to design your retail project. That architect has the skill and aptitude but will have to start low on the learning curve to design a retail project. This is inefficient and expensive. Why should you pay for this learning curve? And you will pay. You must never forget the concept of short-term solvency.

> *"The rule for delegation of responsibility is to use greed, use folly, use intelligence, and use bravery . . . not blaming people for what they are incapable of, but choosing appropriate responsibilities for them according to their respective capacities."*
> —Sun Tzu, sixth century B.C.

Compatibility is essential. You and your development team will work together for many years. You will probably spend more time with your development team than you will with your family and friends. So compatibility of the team members is far more important than skill, aptitude, or experience. You should all like and respect each other. Following this, you all must be able to effectively and regularly communicate with each other. Effective communication is critical. The number one reason why teams fail in any scenario or circumstance is poor communication or lack of communication among its members. How can you attempt to find out if everyone is compatible? There are a number of ways, but here are two examples.

One way is through the use of kickoff meetings. Select your team members as best you can, and then have an official first or kickoff meeting. Actual business is discussed. At the conclusion of this kickoff meeting, you should call and speak to each person in attendance and ask each their opinion of how the meeting went and, one by one, their opinion of each other person in attendance. If there is some hesitation by any team member you are speaking with about another person present at the meeting, even if it is due to that other person's personal habits or style, that criticized team member should immediately be replaced because any hesitation from other team members will inevitably lead to arguments once a project-oriented problem occurs during the development process. A developer has no time for internal squabbles. The old adage of time is money is very applicable in real estate development. On the other hand, constructive criticism is helpful, useful, and wanted. Do not confuse constructive criticism here with what I am essentially describing as personality conflicts.

Another way to test team member compatibility, as someone once described to me, is the two-beer test. Assume, either figuratively or literally, that you have two beers with each individual team member. You try not to discuss business, but instead try to discuss anything else—a casual, relaxed conversation. After these two beers, can you say you have had a good time? Did the person seem like a good person who was able to carry on a conversation? If not, there is likely a compatibility issue, and that team member should be replaced.

As you establish your development team, you should write out your selection criteria for each team member. What type of experience do you want? What type of contractual relationship? You should prepare a simple organizational chart showing the reporting relationships among the team members. You want to write down all of this information for two reasons. First, writing helps you think more clearly and establishes tangible guidelines that anyone can refer to at any time. It will be used as input for your project feasibility report. Second, when—not if—someone leaves your development team, you will have documented your thinking processes and, having done so, will accelerate the process to hire a replacement team member.

So in summary, you will try to have your team organized as shown in Figure 3.1.

FIGURE 3.1   Ideal Development Team

Information flows to and from the developer to each team member. This is the ideal and what every developer strives to achieve. Reality, though, is a bit different. Reality looks something like Figure 3.2.

Nothing happens as planned, and often the appearance of total chaos is evident. However, with proper planning, experience, and compatibility, the team will function more like Figure 3.1.

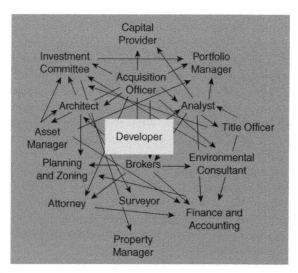

FIGURE 3.2   Realistic Development Team

LEARNING POINTS FROM THIS CHAPTER

After reading this chapter, I should:

- Understand why a development team is necessary.
- Learn who will typically be on your development team.
- Know how to select your development team and assess their abilities.

CHAPTER 4

Historical Perspective of Real Estate Development

History for many people is a dry topic. It is the past. I stated in Chapter 1 that historical trends are useless to a developer. I am not going to contradict myself by including this chapter in the book—at least not completely. My intention in this chapter is not to resurrect thousands of years of history but instead highlight major aspects. If you understand how property development has occurred and does occur, you will be in a good position to establish that trend beyond the trend. If you accept the idea that real estate development in the United States has progressed the furthest of any country, by learning the timeline of real estate development you can then be in a good position to predict what is likely to happen in the future, since everyone else trails the United States. Looking at the United States and its many cities, you can apply this same concept to various other cities in the United States. If arguably cities such as New York, Chicago, and Los Angeles are the most experienced with real estate development, you can apply this timeline to secondary and tertiary cities and towns to identify the trend beyond the trend.

THE BEGINNINGS OF REAL ESTATE DEVELOPMENT

All cities, towns, and villages anywhere in the world have to address five basic concepts.

1. Agricultural base
2. Locational fundamentals and linkages
3. CBD development
4. Building technology
5. Types of conveyance

The Agricultural Base

Villages, towns, and cities anywhere in the world generally begin with agriculture. Farms are established near a water source for two reasons:

1. Irrigation for crops
2. A method of transportation to access the farm and to receive supplies or ship produce to end users

As farms are established, these farms have needs. They need seed, they need machinery, they need fertilizer, and they need skilled labor, among other things. The need providers locate seemingly randomly near the farms. Each need provider creates a way of living for themselves as well as for the farms. The locations of these need providers surrounding the farms exhibit what's called the central place theory. That is, need providers locate around a central place, the farms. See Figure 4.1.

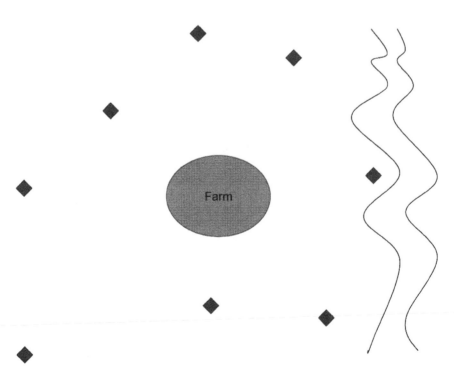

FIGURE 4.1 Central Place Theory

Locational Fundamentals and Linkages

Real estate is still about location, location, location. For a parcel of real estate to be usable, individuals need to have access to that parcel of real estate. The ability of an individual to get from one place to another—point A to point B—is referred to as a linkage. Linkages are extremely important for a parcel of real estate. It is so important that it is correct to say that linkages create inherent value for a parcel. Let me repeat: Linkages create inherent value for a parcel. These transportation links could consist of walking, bicycling, horse riding, car driving, train, or airplane. The more linkages a parcel has, the more inherently valuable is that parcel. The fewer linkages a parcel has, the less value that parcel has. The good news is that you can usually create additional linkages. Let's say a parcel can only be accessed by a footpath. The relative value of that parcel is average. However, if you widen that footpath so a car or truck can be driven on it, the value of the parcel has increased. By adding additional linkages you increase the value further.

Along this same line of thinking, a parcel's proximity to other businesses or employment promotes convenience and creates value. Why does anyone live in a particular town or city? It is because it is convenient to that person's place of employment and because services deemed important by that person are relatively nearby or convenient. Hence a parcel's proximity to employment and other services causes that parcel to be more valuable than a parcel not conveniently located to employment and other services.

Government subsidies can create value for a location. Here subsidies are not limited to money but could include laws and regulations. An abandoned steel mill was unused for many years. The location of the 1,600-acre property is exceptional. It is located near an interstate highway and near an international airport, has rail lines running through the property, and is located near a navigable river. Yet, no developer would develop this property. The city and state were concerned because not only was the site an eyesore but also it was unproductive as far as property tax revenue. Many thought the developers' hesitation was due to obvious contamination issues. Yet, you will learn that environmental contamination is not really a problem. The contamination can be identified, and a plan and budget can be crafted to clean up or eliminate the contamination. Thus the contamination is reduced to a business decision: Can the development budget afford the cost of the cleanup? The real issue is environmental liability. It may never happen, or it could happen that a claim for cancer or birth defects in an area is attributed to this site. The current property owner under U.S. law would be responsible.

The state in which the property is located suddenly became enlightened. They offered to any developer willing to clean up the site contamination at his cost and effort an environmental indemnity. The indemnity would break the ownership chain of title such that the current owner would not be held liable for any future (due to past environmental) contamination activities. Once the state issued this indemnity, a developer quickly took control of the site, created a master plan for about 10 percent of the site, and development is actively occurring. The benefit to the state is that in a few years, it will have a productive tax-paying asset. Government subsidies can create value.

We have been talking about traditional linkages: walking, driving, flying, and the like. The world has advanced in large part today due to the Internet, with many people now working from their homes or other remote locations. As such, the Internet or an Internet connection has become another linkage. When designing a building, it is essential to have the desired Internet access and capabilities; otherwise, you are relinquishing a linkage, thus inherently reducing the value of your property before you have built anything! Linkages create inherent value for a parcel.

CBD Development

Central business districts (CBDs) are employment and retail centers. They grow along the concept of the central place theory. If we consider the hypothetical farm earlier in the chapter, we saw the farm as the center point, with businesses providing materials and services located in proximity to the farm. If we draw lines between the farm and each of the businesses located nearby, these lines represent linkages. The different line lengths represent the different types of linkages. Walking is relatively short, while train riding is relatively long. We have taken the central place theory and matured it into the solar model, where the farm with its emanating linkages looks like a crude depiction of the sun. (See Figure 4.2.) All cities, towns, and villages grow along the linkages available. As an extension of this thought, the growth of a city, town, or village is limited by the linkages available to it. The available linkages cause the transition of land use patterns over time.

Nevertheless, people want to be in a CBD. It is the place where transportation is easy, services are readily available, and there is an available and active social life. As a result, prices of land are relatively very high because of never-ending demand. Strangely, it has been shown, even in the most recent U.S. Census, that the average commute time is 30 minutes.

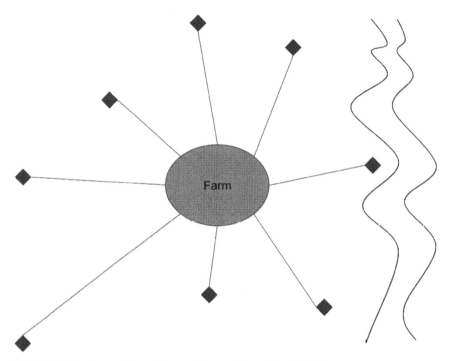

FIGURE 4.2   Central Place Theory Matured into Solar Model

Now, frankly, I don't know of anyone who has only a 30-minute commute, but this statistic is used to define the usefulness or value of a linkage. That is, if using a linkage takes more than 30 minutes, then there must be another linkage or CBD to reduce the average commute time to 30 minutes. Thus, we often end up with edge cities at the ends of linkages. Edge cities are adjacent towns that as they continue to grow, eventually touch each other.

Building Technology

Given the high demand and high value of land in CBDs, developers struggled to devise a solution to increase density in the CBDs. Buildings were limited to about 10 stories because of the building materials available: wood and stone. Above 10 stories, the buildings constructed of these materials were not physically stable. Along comes steel. Steel has stable and flexible characteristics that, when combined with stone (or concrete), allowed developers to build the first skyscrapers. To make them usable, elevators had to be developed. Elevators have been around since the third century B.C., but they lacked a reliable braking system. An American by the name of Elisha Otis equipped an elevator with a safety device to prevent falling in case a supporting cable should break. This increased public confidence in such devices, and as a result, sky-scrapers became useable and popular.

Types of Conveyance

Real estate is comprised of a bundle of rights covering air, surface, and subsurface ownership. There are various forms of ownership in the United States, but the most basic are fee simple ownership and leasehold interest. With fee simple ownership, the property owner has the right to occupy the property, has the right of quiet enjoyment, has the right to sell or assign the property, and has the right to modify the property. With a leasehold interest, the lease holder has the right to occupy the property and the right of quiet enjoyment. The lease holder may or may not have the right to sell or assign a lease (as discussed in a later chapter). Before the United States was established, land ownership was essentially possessory; that is, if you took control of property and, say, placed a fence around it, it was yours. The country was open, and generally no one challenged your right to claim property. This is how property was acquired early on. As the United States further grew from the arrival of colonists from England and elsewhere, land holdings started to expand beyond the CBDs. As we discussed earlier, most people prefer to be in or near a CBD. However, colonists arriving earlier had laid claim to most property located in or near a CBD. Frankly, many of these new landowners had more property than they could use. So, a concept from the British legal system was introduced, land or ground leases. Thus, property was now ground leased to newly arriving colonists allowing them to be in or near CBDs. The earlier colonists, wealthy as a result of acquiring property at no cost, now were charging others rent for the use of the land.

As the United States was established, land continued to be subdivided into parcels to be leased to additional newly arriving colonists. In fact, after the Revolutionary War, the U.S. federal government transferred more than a billion acres to private owners through land sales and grants. Later, in the 1830s, the U.S. federal government sold 20 million acres to private owners for about US\$1.25 per acre. At the time, the majority of citizens could not afford the purchase price. Consequently, a grassroots group called the Free Soil Movement was formed and lobbied the federal government for an alternate method of transferring land into private ownership.

The result was the 1862 Homestead Act. Settlers were given title to 160 acres of land per adult in a family. The understanding was that the settlers would live on, use, and improve the land for a period of at least five years. Improvement constituted establishing a farm, a livestock facility, and so on. At the end of the five years, the settlers would receive full title to their property. The government distributed more than 300 million acres of public property to private landowners and, as a result, created the basis for a real estate market in the United States.

> *"The brave act quickly, while the timid drag their feet. When opponents see you are not moving ahead, they will assume you are timid and will take you lightly."*
>
> —Sun Tzu, sixth century B.C.

Let's jump ahead to the late 1800s. Much growth in the United States was spawned by railroads. This growth, in retrospect, was an early version of what today we call sprawl. Nevertheless, two suburbs built in the United States were unique in their approaches and established lessons still used today. The first was Llewellyn Park, New Jersey. Here the developer subdivided property for building and selling single-family home lots. The developer placed deed restrictions on each of the lots to limit what structures could be built, the size, the materials used, and other factors. In doing so, the developer set a common standard, thus maintaining property values and hopefully increasing market values over time. In other words, if you bought a building lot in Llewellyn Park, you knew that on any side of your property only certain types of buildings (single-family homes) could be built. Someone who bought a lot was guaranteed that no undesirable building, such as commercial uses, stables or garages, or a waste treatment plant, could be put up adjacent your property.

The second example involved Riverside, Illinois, about 15 miles west of the city of Chicago. A developer saw that rail tracks were being built to take passengers to the west of the city. Chicago was fully built, with additional density limited by building technology (at this time, one could construct a building up to only about 10 stories). So the developer said that this land (Riverside) was now viable because the railroad made the area accessible. The railroad was an additional linkage. The developer built a number of single-family homes and marketed to people frustrated by the lack of space in the city of Chicago. While these people would not be in the city proper, they had easy access to and from the city via the railroad. However, the developer experienced something that no one could ever have anticipated in 1871, the great Chicago fire. The city essentially burned to the ground.

Many existing property owners were so discouraged from their loss that they decided to leave the city instead of rebuilding. As a result, property in the city of Chicago suddenly became available, and the development in Riverside failed. Eventually, land in the city was taken up, and nothing was available. Over the next few decades, the city of Chicago and the town of Riverside each grew, and as a result, Riverside, Illinois, became a thriving community.

These suburbs, such as Llewellyn Park and Riverside, were upper-end suburbs built for and used by the wealthy in society—the few who could afford the train tickets and a single-family residence. Single-family homes were mostly bought for cash, and if mortgages were utilized, they were short-term, averaging about six months. Automobiles were becoming visible, and streetcars were built to provide low-cost public transportation within a city. There was a lot of real estate investment occurring, somewhat enhanced by a laissez-faire financial approach to acquiring and owning property.

MAJOR EVENTS CAUSING CHANGE IN THE UNITED STATES

Eight distinct events in the United States caused dramatic change in the way real estate development and investment was perceived and pursued. The first was the Great Depression, starting in 1929. At this time, the U.S. banking system collapsed. Many people lost their jobs. For those who did have short-term mortgages, their homes were foreclosed by the bank. Needless to say, there were major population shifts throughout the country. (Remember that understanding real estate development means that you need to understand people and their movements.) The federal government intervened in the financial markets by forming agencies such as the FHA (Federal Housing Authority). It took about a decade, but World War II, through its need for manufacturing and the resultant employment, eventually and then quickly grew the country out of the depression.

World War II ended in the mid-1940s, with hundreds of thousands of U.S. soldiers returning home and seeking a place to live. During the war, no development really occurred, and there was tremendous pent-up demand for buildings of all property types, especially single-family housing. As a result, towns like Levittown, New York (and many, many others throughout the United States), were created by using manufactured homes. The manufactured homes could be erected very quickly and for a very affordable price. As in any overheated, high-demand economy, the manufacturers started taking shortcuts and using lower-quality materials so the houses could be shipped and built even faster. As a result of the poor quality control, many of the manufactured homes physically collapsed, causing market failure.

> *"Ten years ago, everybody had had enough with real estate investments. Now foreign investors and newcomers to the real estate market who have not had their fingers burnt are rushing in without thinking of potential risks."*
> —Yasuo Ide, analyst and owner, real estate investment research company, *Taipei Times*, March 28, 2005

Coupled with the market failure were the Cold War tensions, and at this time, the 1950s, the U.S. interstate highway system was built at the direction of President Eisenhower. Although the interstate highway system was originally built for military purposes (Cold War), it became very popular for automobile travel. The interstate highway system clearly exacerbated sprawl and the suburbanization of the United States.

Suburbanization clearly affected the American landscape. New housing was being built everywhere, funded in part by the FHA—the federal government. Automobiles were becoming more prevalent in households, and there was a huge population shift out to the new suburbs. As an aside, the interstate highway system alone did not bring about the growth of suburbs. There was a more important motivation. The cities were getting old and rundown. People flocked to the suburbs for newly built housing and less congestion. Nevertheless, the majority of jobs were still in the city, and people did have to commute from their homes. The average at the time for the preferred maximum commute was 30 minutes. (Strangely, 30 minutes is still the average commute time.) With the new suburbs being created and expanded, multinucleus patterns developed. That is, instead of being a conglomeration of single-family homes, suburbs were being designed and built to look like mini-cities that had housing, office buildings, retail space, industrial property, hotels— all the property types typically found in any city.

As people continued migrating to the suburbs, the city urban areas were left in transition. Buildings were no longer fully occupied and, as mentioned before, were old and often undesirable. With people leaving the cities, property values dropped, as did tax revenues. This caused cities

to experience budget shortfalls, resulting in reductions or cutbacks in services. Some governments, using their police powers, assembled various
small parcels into one large parcel, with the hope that private developers
would take notice, propose a major project, and thus replace some of the
city's lost tax revenues. This approach was not always effective, as evi-
denced in St. Louis, Missouri. Here the city assembled land and offered
the larger parcel to any developer who would demolish the existing structures and rebuild. A developer expressed interest in the city's proposal.
The developer indeed demolished the existing buildings, but when faced
with the decision to rebuild, the developer had second thoughts. The developer looked around and could not justify building a new project because, frankly, there were no people around who at the time would be
attracted by such a new project. As a result, the developer left the city and
left behind a large area flattened by demolition that was known as Hiro-
shima Flats, (implying that the area looked similar to the city in Japan
after the atomic bombing).

With the cities losing tax revenues, those who remained in the city—
those who could not afford to relocate to the wealthy and expensive suburbs—became frustrated, resulting in the urban crisis of the 1960s. It was a
tumultuous time during the 1960s in America, with urban riots and people
such as Martin Luther King Jr., President Kennedy, and his brother Senator
Kennedy being assassinated. Private developers had no interest in working
in the cities, and those who did abandoned their projects to work in the
suburbs.

The federal government, acknowledging the severe problems in cities,
created HUD, the Department of Housing and Urban Development. HUD
built many of what we now recognize as the bland, monolithic apartment
buildings. When these towers were first built, they were highly successful
endeavors providing housing, bringing some people back into the city, and
mitigating the loss of tax revenues.

Nevertheless, the suburbs continued to grow and grew faster as the
urban crisis of the 1960s continued. New property types came into existence, such as motels or motor hotels; shopping centers, a conglomeration
of individual retail stores into one physical site or building; and office and
industrial parks, all of which were applications of the multinuclei concept.
While many new suburbs or planned new towns were being built, three
are particularly notable. The first is Shaker Heights, Ohio. Here a developer was hoping to assemble various tracts of land to build a planned
new town. As he spoke with the landowners, these farmers could not understand why a developer would be interested in their land. The developer
offered option contracts and was willing to pay the landowners to obtain
those rights. The farmers were so dismayed by the developer's motivation

that the farmers gave purchase options to the developer but refused to accept any payment. Thus, the land for what was to become Shaker Heights, one of the country's most affluent suburbs, was assembled by using no-cost options.

The second notable suburb was Columbia, Maryland, just outside Baltimore. Columbia was, and I believe still is, the largest land assemblage in the United States to date. Columbia was developed by Rouse Co., a real estate development company that utilized basic multinuclei concepts. Now Columbia, Maryland, is home to approximately 97,000 people.

The third notable suburb is Reston, Virginia, which was supposedly the largest single land acquisition in the United States. Readers may find the irony in the following. This single land acquisition was made by a developer from an oil company. During the early twentieth century in the United States, many saw these newfangled contraptions with four wheels called cars traveling throughout the country. The oil companies started to think that these cars were probably going to be successful. As a result, the oil companies started acquiring land throughout the country for future oil drilling purposes. As a result, the oil companies were probably the third largest landowner in the country, behind the federal government and the railroads. In the late 1960s and 1970s, despite the oil crisis of the 1970s, Middle East oil was very inexpensive and incredibly plentiful. The oil companies then decided that it would be a waste of their balance sheets holding all of this property for future drilling. So in the case of Reston, Virginia, the oil company sold its land holdings to a developer in the 1980s. The land area is so large that Reston, Virginia, is still being developed decades later.

The U.S. government was very much on board with promoting real estate development throughout the United States. The federal government established a number of programs to encourage more and more investment. Despite the federal government's enthusiasm toward promoting real estate investment, banks were further regulated so that the experience of the late 1920s (the Depression) would not be revisited, and savings and loans would be protected after failure. Additional agencies such as Fannie Mae and Freddie Mac were also established to expand the secondary mortgage markets throughout the country, which provided a vehicle giving additional liquidity to the banks. Secondary mortgage markets had existed for many years, but trades were done on a relatively informal basis. Fannie Mae and Freddie Mac were established to grow and institutionalize the secondary mortgage trading business. Real estate was also favored under the tax code. The Internal Revenue Service offered real estate investors a number of tax credits and programs, again to encourage more and more real estate investment throughout the country.

"In this business, without an ego you're not going to get anywhere."
—Peter Solomon, Coachella Valley, California, developer, (Riverside, Calif.) *Press Enterprise*, April 9, 2005

However, as in any market that becomes overheated, the government had to establish various fair housing laws. The 1968 Fair Housing Act, as modified, stated that there will be no discrimination on the basis of race, color, religion, or national origin. In addition, the law stated that there would be no discrimination for various protected groups. The government was trying to offset a common practice called redlining, often used by banks to mark areas of the map where the bank would not lend. This action by itself is not illegal. It's done by banks every day. What made this illegal under this new law is that while banks would not lend into certain areas marked off by a red line, they would continue to take deposits. Redlining almost never happens today. The other practice that became prevalent is called blockbusting, which is distinguished by the use of scare tactics to get property owners to sell. This scare tactic often used to say that property values will decline because of a certain racial or religious group moving into the area. Blockbusting is illegal. However, a person can be convicted of blockbusting not by breaking the law, but just by the implication that the person will break the law. The implication is tested by agents of the federal government. For example, a couple representing themselves to be looking for a house in a particular area may ask a Realtor to not show them neighborhoods that might contain certain racial or religious groups. The Realtor should only state that he or she cannot do that. Saying something like "No problem, I understand" is the implication that constitutes a violation under the blockbusting law.

One exception to the points mentioned in the previous paragraphs is the Community Reinvestment Act (CRA), which requires that federally chartered banks in the United States must lend into economically stressed areas if they are to maintain their federal banking charter and do business throughout the country. The banks are given budgets for the amount to lend into these economically distressed areas. This law is currently being criticized by the public as being an example of practices that contributed to the credit crisis in 2008, that is, making required loans to individuals or companies that perhaps do not qualify for loans. Nevertheless, from a practical perspective, if you as a developer would like to do a project in a pioneering area that is economically stressed, the first bank you should visit is a CRA lender. These lenders want to lend to you as long as your project makes sense and your credit is good.

In this short chapter, I have outlined a little history of real estate development in the United States. Again, the idea is that if you understand the timeline, you can then overlay the timeline on any city in the United States or anywhere else in the world. A later chapter of this book picks up in the 1970s and 1980s, when we left off here, and continues on to today.

LEARNING POINTS FROM THIS CHAPTER

After reading this chapter, I should:

- Understand how villages, towns, and cities grow through their linkages.
- Understand how a city is designed via the multinuclei concept.
- Have an understanding of how a government can help or hurt real estate development.
- Start to understand how studying history can help in formulating the trend beyond the trend.

CHAPTER 5

Market Research

In this chapter, we begin discussing functional areas addressed within the development process. My intention is not to teach you how to do market research; many books and university classes can teach you the basic and advanced concepts of market research. Instead, my intention is to discuss how a real estate developer looks at and uses market research for pursuing a development project.

INCEPTION OF THE IDEA

The inception of the idea begins with an unsatisfied need in a market or on an underutilized existing site. How does one come up with an idea for a development site? This is a challenge for every developer, but let's discuss the concept of an unsatisfied need. Often you will find that many people do not know what they want or what they're missing. It's that negative approach I mentioned before—that if you tried to determine what someone really wants, it would be difficult, if not impossible. On the other hand, if you try to determine what a person does not want to do or is not doing, coming up with an idea is easier.

There was a book published a few years ago called *Blue Ocean Strategy* (*Blue Ocean Strategy: How to Create Uncontested Market Space and Make the Competition Irrelevant*, by W. Chan Kim and Renée Mauborgne; Harvard Business School Press, 2005). Its premise is that a market is an open, blue ocean. Picture a blue ocean in your mind, which is what the authors argue is the market a company should pursue. The opposite of the blue ocean in business is the red ocean, which is bloody from competition. Imagine in this metaphor an ocean filled with sharks trying to get ahead by attacking each other. This is what many companies do. They look at their competitors' products and try to copy what their competitors are doing, possibly making small changes to create a distinctive product. The authors of *Blue Ocean Strategy* argue that doing business in a red ocean is a waste of time and money. Nothing really new or innovative is created. On the other hand, doing business in the blue ocean offers tremendous opportunities. Without going into details, the authors state that there are two distinct characteristics of a company that uses a blue ocean strategy. One is that the company often can't be pigeonholed into a particular industry. An example the authors use is the Cirque du Soleil. What business are they really in? The second characteristic of a company that uses the blue ocean strategy is that essentially the company has no competition. Again consider the Cirque du Soleil. So the idea is that a company using a blue ocean strategy perhaps straddles several industries and has no direct competition—well, you can see the benefits.

Enough talk about generic companies. A real estate developer needs to analyze the market and then identify a particular need or segment niche whose needs are not being filled by existing buildings. With this in mind as you start to do market research, you should be looking again for the negative. What's not there? If you're building an office building in an office campus area, what services do not exist? If, for example, you notice that none of the office buildings in the immediate area has a deli in the lobby, perhaps this is an amenity that should be included in your proposed project that will distinguish it as the only building with such an amenity resulting in added value. As a result, you should be able to request higher rent.

MARKETS, MARKET RESEARCH, AND MARKETING (ANALYSIS OF DEVELOPMENT POTENTIAL)

This section talks about market research for marketing your project. Frankly, that's what you're trying to do when you properly perform market research is marketing. Remember the first three questions from the enterprise concept: What are you doing? Whom are you doing it for? Whom are you affecting? Before we get into too much detail, let's again set some parameters for discussion.

There are two purposes for market study: due diligence and political reasons.

There is a good chance that most of you reading this book have used the due diligence rationale for market study. Often you receive a deal book or a book of information from a broker who is trying to sell you a site. You then review the information and perhaps do a simple financial analysis to determine if the project makes sense for you. Once you complete this analysis and you're positively inclined toward pursuing the project, you need to review your key assumptions with actual market data. Testing that data against the market data attempts to ensure that you are making a prudent and informed decision. Frankly, this is something that a developer does every single day. After comparing the assumptions against the market data, you may find that you need to modify the assumptions and recalculate your financial analysis.

The second rationale for a market study is for political purposes. What does this mean? You hope to accomplish three things: to develop further interest in a worthy project, to gather the local consensus, and to justify public expenditures. A key aspect of doing a market study is not to sit at a computer terminal or pore over directories to gather your market data. While this is necessary to a certain extent, talking to people produces the most valuable market data. You as a developer *must* go into the market and start asking questions of the local citizens (one of your many constituencies) and develop interest in your project. Granted, some of the people you speak with will have some negative comments, but that is not a problem because you are in fact gathering market data or information. This information is incredibly valuable to you as a developer, because as long as you incorporate that data, information, desires, needs, and wants into your project concept, the people you speak to will start to be interested and supportive. As you include this information into your project design concept, you in effect will start to solidify local consensus. That is, people will start to think that your idea, with their input, is a project they would like to see happen within their community. So at this stage, you have accomplished two of the three reasons of doing market research for political purposes. The last reason is to justify public expenditures. What public expenditures? Remember that every time you do a new development or redevelopment project, you cause change. You may be adding to the traffic flow, creating additional noise, causing strain on the school system, or stressing the infrastructure in the city or town. Who pays for these changes? Needless to say, the government pays for these additional costs through incremental tax revenues from the various existing and new projects. So as you go into the market, talk to the community, spark their interest, and produce a local consensus, you must also be speaking with the government (another one of your constituencies) explaining how your project will generate the incremental tax revenues to justify the expenditures necessary. If you make your argument clearly, you help the government justify the necessary public expenditures.

In short, the most valuable purpose of the market study is the political purpose because here you as a developer truly begin the entitlement process, that is, the process by which you get the approvals you need to build your prospective project. I also want to point out, as I did earlier, and emphasize that the quantitative data associated with the traditional market research approach is not as important as talking to people.

Now that we understand the purposes of a market study, we need to understand the market players. Who are they? Essentially, the market players are the groups that you will sell to, first of all the end users or tenants who will lease or buy the space of your proposed project. Once again, you need to understand their needs and wants. If you are designing and building a project for them, the next market players you need to be concerned about are the buyers. I'm not talking about the buyers of space such as condominiums. The buyers in this case are the buyers of the property. At some point, you will sell your project. Whether you sell your project once you complete it and lease it up or sell it 5, 10, or 15 years from now, you need to have a good idea of who will be the eventual buyer of your property. Will it be another developer, or perhaps a REIT? Let's say you want to be a builder of water parks. You do a very good job at developing, constructing and operating water parks. However, you decide you want to sell a water park. Who would buy it? I think this would be a very difficult question to answer. Frankly, it would be easier to sell a prison, because there is at least one REIT that owns and operates prisons. This is a repeat of what I said earlier; as a developer, you build buildings for others. You do not build a project for yourself. To be a bit brutal, no one cares what you think. Your opinion is meaningless because what really matters is what your end users, tenants, and buyers of the property are interested in.

The last market players are the users. Many developers often do not think about the users, the clients of your end users or tenants. They are the customers of retail stores in a shopping center; they go to the office buildings to visit their accountants or attorneys. How do these users get to your property? How do they view your property from an aesthetic standpoint? Once again, linkages are incredibly important. Let's say you develop an outstandingly designed building, but it is difficult to get to that building; it will clearly have a difficult time leasing up. Another user who is incredibly important to your end user is the end user's employees. Your end user tenant is very concerned about the qualified job pool that surrounds the building where you would like the business to lease space. In New York City prior to September 11, 2001, many financial companies had their back office operations in lower Manhattan. Following 9/11, these financial companies decided that it was shortsighted to have too much of their business located on the island of Manhattan. Many of them moved their back office operations across the Hudson River to cities like Jersey City, New Jersey. When these financial companies moved their back office operations across the river, according to newspaper articles they lost as many as 50 percent of their employees. Why? It was a matter of linkages. Before the move, most employees only had to take a subway to get to work. Now these employees had to take a subway, get off, and then take a PATH train or a ferry to get to Jersey City. This made the employees' commute not only more time-consuming but also more expensive. So a developer, when selecting a site and designing a building to be built on that site, has to consider not only the end user tenant but also the clients and employees of an end user. If the end user does not feel that your building and its location are convenient for clients and employees, the end user is not going to lease space within your building.

Now what is a market? Many market researchers define a market by drawing concentric circles around a particular site as the market that will be attracted by a property. Well, I think is important to understand a definition of a market. A market is all the potential customers sharing a particular need or want who might be willing and able to engage in exchange to satisfy that need or want. Who would be considered potential customers sharing a particular need or want? Consider developing a shopping center. The news of your efforts goes out into the market (mainly because you've been talking to the market about your proposed project). You are approached by a Hallmark store owner-operator. He says to you that he is very interested in your new shopping center because it is new, it is well located, and it has tremendous traffic and visibility. Clearly, this Hallmark store owner-operator is a potential customer who is sharing a particular need or want for your project. The Hallmark store owner-operator should be considered part of your targeted market. But is he willing and able? Well, he is willing because he is telling you he is willing because he's attracted by the location and visibility. But is he able? As you continue to have a conversation with this Hallmark store owner-operator, you learn that he just signed a 10-year lease at another property last week. Is he able to come to your property? Perhaps, but not likely. If the Hallmark store owner-operator decides he wants to break his 10-year lease, I suspect that the lease cancellation penalty payment would be a major disincentive. So, the Hallmark store owner-operator is not able. Thus, he should be eliminated from your targeted market. Let's say you have been speaking to a number of prospective tenants. Are these tenants willing to engage in exchange? What is being exchanged here? Of the two things being exchanged, space is one. You have the space, clearly. The prospective tenant will exchange money for the space. Does the prospective tenant have the money? This is the purpose of credit checks and financial underwriting. A prospective tenant might really like your property, but that prospective tenant may not be able to afford your property. A prospective tenant who cannot afford your property must be eliminated from your targeted market. So, you see, a market cannot merely be a series of concentric circles around the site. You must have much further insight into a market to be able to understand how that market can help you and your project.

CONCEPTS THAT DEFINE MARKETING (AND MARKETS)

Marketing and market research is a social and managerial process. It is a social process, of course, because you as a developer should be constantly talking to people and understanding the needs and wants of the people you speak to. It is a managerial process because based on the information and knowledge you learn, you will further define your idea. Identifying people's needs and wants is absolutely critical and essential. If you do not understand what the needs and wants are for your various constituencies, your project at best will be mediocre and clearly not of the highest value. And again, value creation is the ultimate goal of the developer.

The next concept that defines marketing is creating a notion of value and assuring the satisfaction of expectations. First, let's look at this phrase "notion of value." This is an incredibly important concept for you as a developer to understand. It goes back to my earlier comment that it really doesn't matter what you think. It's all about the needs and wants of your targeted market and constituencies. Let's think hypothetically about this situation. Let's say that there are two apartment buildings. The apartment buildings are absolutely identical. They are the same size, they have the same finishes, and they are so identical, they exist in the same physical space—ridiculous, I know, but work with me here. The only difference between the two apartment buildings is that one apartment building has Formica countertops in the kitchen and the other apartment building has granite countertops in the kitchen. Which apartment building is more valuable? Many would say that the apartment building with the granite countertops is more valuable. But is it really? What's the purpose of a kitchen countertop? You can chop vegetables on both countertops, Formica and granite, the same way with the same results. Why would the apartment building with granite countertops be considered more valuable? Some would argue that the granite for the kitchen countertop is more expensive and long-lasting and thus should be more valuable. This perception exhibits the notion of value. Perception is reality. It doesn't matter what you think; it matters what your end user thinks. The notion of value is what you as a developer are trying to identify from your conversations with your prospective target market. Learning the many notions of values of your prospective target market is essential as you begin to select your site and assign a building on your chosen site. Of course, you have to create a satisfaction of expectations. If your prospective target market has a notion of value of some aspect of your proposed project, you need to satisfy that expectation. Otherwise, your prospective target market will not be an end user for your project. Last, as we highlighted in the definition of a market, the developer must instigate an exchange of space for money.

Real estate is a product. It is no different than a tube of toothpaste or a gallon of bleach. All are highly differentiated (different flavors or aromas), just like office buildings are all different from each other. All have variable supply constraints and have to deal with uncertain market data. No one ever knows exactly where demand is for their product. All are highly customized. But real estate has an unusual focus that distinguishes it from all other products, entitlements. Who is entitled? Not the developer. It is the government and the community.

Entitlements are extremely important to a developer. At this stage in the development process, your efforts will be devoted to securing local and political approvals. Remember that I mentioned that market research and marketing is a social process? You need to do societal marketing (community and government) to obtain these approvals. If you do not, your project will never be realized. I often read about or speak to developers who complain about how difficult a government and a community are acting by asking too many questions or requiring various changes in projects that cause a developer frustration and stress. I listen to these rants and then ask a question: Did you [the developer] have a conversation with the community or the government prior to seeking the official approvals? In all cases, the answer is no. If the developer had simply had a conversation with his constituencies, gathering interest and consensus, the developer would not have the difficulties he is complaining about.

Ask questions. How (do entitlement approvals occur)? Who (should I be speaking to)? What (needs to be done)? When (does the process occur)? We ask these questions in preparation for the public-private partnership, a partnership that is essential for any developer who wants to have a successful and relatively straightforward project. To be successful, a developer must respond to the government's plans for a community. Rather than deciding on a project *you* want to build, talk to the city. Ask them what they would like to see built in the city. Two experiences immediately come to mind. A development group had thoughts of building a multifamily project in a town. The developer was enlightened enough to schedule a meeting with the town's mayor to discuss his plans. At the meeting, the mayor patiently listened and then said that he was not interested in another residential project. The mayor said he was far more interested in building commercial projects, with the desire to increase the town's overall tax base and to reduce the tax bills for existing residential property owners. Over a few weeks, the developer took the mayor's comments to heart. Since the developer learned after speaking with people that the majority of the town's residents were elderly, the developer decided to build an office building and a high-rise assisted-living facility essentially compromising the mayor's and developer's desires. In one plan, the developer addressed the mayor's desire for commercial buildings by proposing an office building (assisted living is considered commercial) and included a residential building (people do live in assisted-living facilities). The mayor, when reviewing the developer's revised proposal, was ecstatic and supported the developer's request for approval with the planning board.

Another story involves a developer again speaking with a town's mayor. Understanding the mayor's desires from initial and preliminary meetings, the developer designed a large mixed-use project. The developer then decided to have a follow-up meeting with the mayor to preview his project plan. The mayor was excited and enthusiastic about the proposed project. But he had one request. Would the developer take the project as designed and relocate it to a site about one to two blocks away?

What do you think was the developer's response? What do you think should have been the developer's response? The answer to both questions is the same. The developer said that he would be happy to, as long as the recommended site was available and was of substantially the same characteristics as the originally planned site, that is, acquisition cost, soil and environmental attributes, and the like (and it was). By responding this way, the developer heard the mayor's subliminal message. The mayor was in essence telling the developer that if the developer would move the project to the recommended site, the mayor would support the project. If the developer did not move his proposed project to the recommended site, then the mayor would not support the project. As far as the developer is concerned, he will still earn the same developer's fee and probably have the same project financial return—and now will have the mayor's support! The message here is simple and clear. To be successful, a developer must respond to a government's plans for the community.

USING MARKET STUDIES AND PREPARING FOR MARKETABILITY STUDIES

Before starting market research, it is important to understand the flow of activities in Figure 5.1. The first step is the market analysis. A market analysis is quantitative. It gathers quantitative data about a market. The next step is the marketability study. A marketability study (discussed later in this chapter) is one of the most important things you can do because it rationalizes the aspects of a proposed project with the needs and wants of a targeted market. The last step in the flow of market research

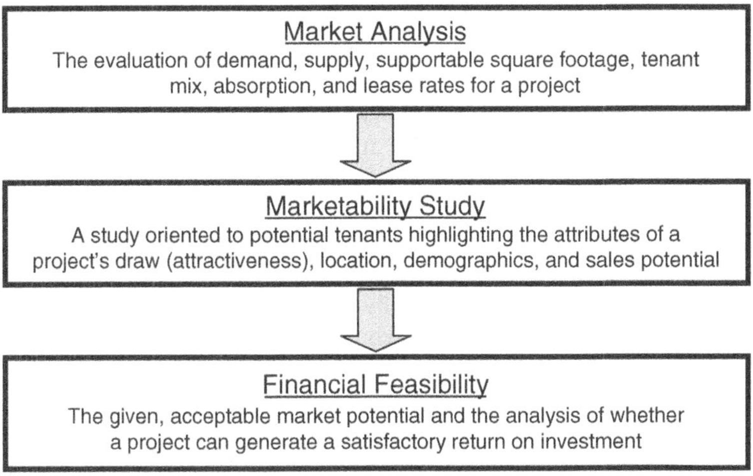

Market Analysis
The evaluation of demand, supply, supportable square footage, tenant mix, absorption, and lease rates for a project

Marketability Study
A study oriented to potential tenants highlighting the attributes of a project's draw (attractiveness), location, demographics, and sales potential

Financial Feasibility
The given, acceptable market potential and the analysis of whether a project can generate a satisfactory return on investment

FIGURE 5.1 The Flow of the Market Research

is to take the data and conclusions reached from the market analysis and the market study and prepare a financial feasibility study. The financial feasibility study uses the quantitative data from the market study (rental rates, expenses, absorption, etc.) and conclusions from the marketability study (choice of property type, overall design, features, etc.). Once again, financial feasibility is one of the last things to consider when working on a development project.

Studying competitive supply is important. Here I disagree slightly with the authors of the *Blue Ocean Strategy*. The authors say that you should ignore the competition and devise an original concept. In the real estate business, it is suicide to ignore the competition. You are trying to create a notion of value, and you will not learn what that is unless you evaluate what is being offered by the competition.

> *"Everybody talks about being over-retailed, but really, the problem is we are under-demolished. A lot of poor properties shouldn't continue."*
> —John Bucksbaum, CEO of General Growth Properties, at the Zell-Lurie Real Estate Center, April 25, 2003

While studying competitive supply, your market analysis starts with an inventory of relevant existing and proposed occupied and vacant space within your designated market area. To begin, you need to determine your market areas. Understand that as you gather information, you will revise the boundaries frequently. As you gather market and competitive information and have preliminary ideas, you should perform a market niche analysis. A market niche analysis tries to assess whether your ideas for a use or tenant are supportable by the market conditions or dynamics. For example, you might think that you would like to have a 10,000-square-foot fast-food restaurant, but looking at the competition, no fast-food restaurant is larger than 3,000 square feet. Is your fast-food restaurant concept unique, specifically addressing the needs and wants of your targeted market? If so, you would have created a notion of value and added an aspect to your spatial monopoly (more on spatial monopolies later).

You should recognize that when using market and marketability studies, you must be cognizant that what you read may not be correct. Why would it not be correct? Well, there are several reasons. The first is an inadequate or ill-defined scope or scope definition. Let's say you want to put up an office building in Chicago. You contact a market research firm and tell them you would like a study of the viability of an office building in Chicago. You say nothing more. How useful do you think the market information you receive will be to you and your proposed office building project? How useful do you think that "Chicago" market information will be to you? Isn't your building going to go in a specific location, such as downtown, west side, Magnificent Mile, or River North? Generic information about the Chicago office market is totally useless to you, yet developers—every day—rely on this generic market information to make decisions about proposed and existing buildings in specific areas of Chicago. Granted, you may not yet know the precise location of your proposed project, but you can better define the scope so it has some possibility of being useful to you.

The second reason often involves environmental realities that should be addressed in a market study. Environmental realities in this context are not about contamination. For example, the market data gathered may be excellent and support the concept of your new project. However, no mention or consideration is given to an election where the leading candidate is openly opposed to new real estate developments in town. So, if this person is elected, no matter how good and supportive the data may be for your proposed project, you will have difficulty getting your project approved. Last, you must consider the concept of GIGO (Garbage In, Garbage Out). If the data gathered is weak or irrelevant, the conclusions reached will be weak or irrelevant.

> *"[Self-storage facilities] have become the attic, the basement, the backroom of America. It's amazing what people will store. It's truly amazing. We are all procrastinators, so goods at rest tend to stay at rest."*
> —Charles Barbo, CEO of Shurgard Storage Centers, at the 26th annual Real Estate and Economics Symposium, sponsored by the Fisher Center for Real Estate and Urban Economics at the University of California at Berkeley, Nov. 20, 2003

If you are starting to get a sense of my cynicism by reading this last paragraph, you're right. I think one of the most valuable characteristics of a developer is good use of cynicism. Cynicism can be put to good use with the understanding that any study, including a market study, could have fatal flaws. One of these fatal flaws, again, includes a poor definition of the market scope. For example, let's say you would like to build an office building in Los Angeles. You proceed and commission a consultant to do a market study by telling him that you would like a market study of Los Angeles for the purpose of building an office building. The consultant is more than willing to do the work. You get the report of the office market in Los Angeles. How useful is that report? It is not really that useful, because Los Angeles is made up of a variety of neighborhoods. You are going to build an office building in a specific neighborhood. Thus you should have requested a market study with a market definition specifying a specific neighborhood or neighborhoods. Surprisingly, many market studies consist of broad market scope definitions, and developers use these market studies to make serious investment decisions. Now, realistically, while you want to build an office building in Los Angeles, you have not quite decided which neighborhood you would like to build in. This is a common dilemma. This means simply that you would start with an overview of the various neighborhoods, and then select a neighborhood to do a more detailed market study.

Another fatal flaw of market studies is not recognizing the environmental realities or political environment. For example, a market study is done that has a fantastic conclusion strongly supporting the construction of an office building. However, the consultant preparing the market study ignores or overlooks the fact that there is a political election in the next year. As part of that political election, the front runner has stated as part of his election platform that he is totally opposed to any new development in his town. As a result, even though you have received a very favorable market study, you will not be able to do a development because of the political opposition.

Then there is the overall fatal flaw called GIGO or garbage in, garbage out. If the data used for the market study is flawed or weak, then any conclusions or results cited by the market study are worthless. Again, all three of these flaws occur on a daily basis. Worse, many real estate developers use these reports with these flaws to pursue significant real estate development projects.

SOURCES OF AND METHODS FOR GATHERING INFORMATION

There are a number of selected data sources that can be used to gather information for a market study: the U.S. Department of Commerce, which has a census of retail trade, a census of service industries, and a survey of current business, for example; the Bureau of the Census for a census of population and housing (www.census.gov); and the Bureau of Labor Statistics, which issues the consumer expenditure survey.

In addition to the public sources, there are various private data services such as the ULI's (Urban Land Institute) *Dollars and Cents*, IREM (Institute of Real Estate Management) income and expense analysis reports, and customized consumer demand surveys. Let's focus here on consumer demand surveys, which are sometimes called focus groups. A survey of consumers is extremely compelling information for investors. The consumer data derived can be useful in increasing the attractiveness of a building or shopping center to end users and their clients and employees. In the case of shopping centers, consumer demand surveys might determine the demand for individual store types and established linkages. As anyone knows who has participated in a consumer demand survey, participants are peppered with a variety of questions. After successfully completing a consumer demand survey, participants are often given a reward such as a discount coupon, a free meal, or sometimes cash. If a participant becomes bored or loses interest while participating in the consumer demand survey, the participant may provide the responses that the questioner wants to hear. So, asking people to project hypothetical behavior often may be unreliable. Similarly, data gathering—that is, finding answers to questions—should consider sampling issues. While consumer demand surveys are still being used on a regular basis, a far more reliable approach that results in the same desired outcome is the use of marketability studies. We will define and talk about the use of marketability studies later.

FLAWS OF A STUDY

We spoke earlier about the fatal flaws of any study. There are additional circumstances that often cause incorrect conclusions of studies, one of which is the conflict of interest or the ethical issues regarding the independence of consultants. For example, when deciding to pursue a project within a new market, you most likely will inquire about who would be a good consultant to use. As a result, you will receive the names of consultants who are widely used within that market. You engage one of those consultants to do a study. The consultants in doing their job will include your proposed project in this database. A database is the most valuable resource to a consultant. Later when this consultant does a project for one of the established developers in town, the established developer sees that there is a proposed project outlined in his study report. At this point, your proposed project has become public information. Is the situation preventable or avoidable? No, not really. You should just be aware that the situation exists and plan accordingly.

Another circumstance involves the purpose of the study. Studies often have two purposes: They either speak the truth or conform to the desired answer. Which purpose is used depends on the developer and the developer's situation. If the developer is trying to learn about a new market, he obviously is trying to seek the truth and is open-minded about any information or conclusions reached. However, many developers get fairly involved and progress much further in the development process before commissioning a market study. Coupled with issues of short-term solvency and a project that must proceed, it becomes very clear to the consultants that the developer wants a report that substantiates the conclusions the developer has already reached—rightly or wrongly. So, if you as a new developer are reviewing several market studies, which one of the two are you looking at? You simply don't know. Again, the characteristic of cynicism comes to bear. Question everything you read, and make your own independent decision.

A common circumstance involves short-term solvency, where the developer allocates a budget amount that is too low for the expected scope of work of a study. A consultant often knows the circumstance when he is presented with it. Market studies vary widely in price. But given the scope from the developer, the consultant can clearly discern that the amount of money the developer wants to pay for the study is deficient. Nevertheless, the consultant still takes the developer's money. However, what will result is a boilerplate report. The consultant will take an old market study and do some minor updates and/or some peripheral research on the Internet and then submit the report for the amount of money paid.

Clearly, my cynicism regarding market research reports comes through in this chapter. I am not saying that you should not have a market study done.

I am saying that you should question everything that is presented to you and make the decision that is best for you and your project.

While I have talked about the flaws of market research reports, there are some characteristics of a good market study. Clearly, a good market study uses the best and most reliable available data. However, be sure that whatever data are used reflects any recent trends or perceived trends. Also, a good market study should detail as many assumptions as possible, making them explicit. With explicit detailed assumptions, changes in the conclusions of the report can be made by changing the assumptions when any changes in the trends or information presented in the report occur after the report is issued. Also, any conclusions reached by a market study should present the conclusions in a range. It amazes me even today that some market researchers make a conclusion by giving absolute numbers or percentages. By giving absolute numbers or percentages, is the market researcher saying that these are guaranteed conclusions? Of course not. That is impossible. So the conclusions should be given in ranges. Be sure to look for this characteristic.

VALIDATE THE DATA AND THE IMPORTANCE OF REVISIONS AND UPDATES

After receiving and reviewing the market study data, be sure to audit the data to make sure the information is rational. Make sure, for example, that the annual change in square footage (new inventory) equals that year's completions, less deletions in inventory. As mentioned earlier, understand the limits of the sample survey, and then think about how the sample has changed by way of changes and trends. If the conclusions are not updated for trends, then the data will be misleading and cause you to make wrong decisions.

LEARNING POINTS FROM THIS CHAPTER

After reading this chapter, I should:

- Understand the purposes of a market study from a developer's perspective.
- Ask questions of all situations, and be cynical.
- Avoid following known trends, but instead search for unidentified trends, that is, unmet needs and wants.

CHAPTER 6

Marketability Studies

Marketability studies are one of the three most important and relevant sections of any feasibility study. As a rule, if the marketability study is not properly written, your idea for a proposed project has not been fully thought out. I often use this quote to explain this concept: "If you cannot sell me on your project's need and want, then you cannot sell me on your concept." In this situation, the *me* is each of your five constituencies.

1. The government.
2. The community.
3. The end users (tenants or buyers).
4. The investors (debt and equity).
5. You, the developer.

The needs and wants of each one of these constituencies must be addressed as part of your marketability study.

SHOWING THAT YOUR DEVELOPMENT CONCEPT COULD AND SHOULD BE BUILT

A marketability study is the measurement of demand for real estate projects for a *specific* project and a *specific* site. The marketability study attempts to prove your idea *could* and *should* be realized. Let's discuss the "could and should" of a project. When we say a project could be built, we are talking about the physical and legal aspects of the project. Are there any physical characteristics such as soil conditions, environmental contamination, or topography that could physically prevent or impair the construction of your planned project? Are there any laws or regulations such as zoning requirements that could prevent or impair the overall design or scope of your planned project? Often, many of these restrictions and impairments can be identified by doing a site constraint analysis or by completing the elements of design as discussed in Chapter 7. This analysis is often referred to as the site constraint analysis. In a site constraint analysis, you show the constraints associated with a project site, such as physical constraints or legal constraints. After identifying site constraints, the marketability study outlines the solutions for these constraints, hopefully concluding that you *could* build the project.

Once you have thoroughly analyzed your capability of physically building the project that you want to build, you should investigate the *should* of the project. That is, should the project be built? The *should* of the project addresses the needs and wants of your target market and generally your constituencies, compared with the property type, features, and amenities of the building you plan to build. Is this the appropriate property type? Are you offering the necessary amenities that are attractive to your target market? Is your target market willing to pay for the proposed features and amenities? These are some of the questions that you will ask in trying to define the *should* of a proposed project. A marketability study should strive to answer these questions:

- Will there be end users to rent or buy your proposed project?
- How quickly, and at what rent or price, will your proposed project be absorbed into the market?
- How might your proposed project be planned or marketed to make it more competitive in its market?

Once you believe you have reached a first draft of a marketability study, compare your project's concept with competitive properties in the market. Be sure to answer the question of whether there is sufficient demand for your proposed project, given anticipated absorption and capture rates. Be sure your project meets the needs and wants of your defined target market. As you do this analysis, you actually start to prepare your marketing plan. As part of your marketing plan, you will decide whether you will market your proposed project by comparing its amenities or its pricing with the competition. The reality is that a project cannot be marketed on both its amenities and its pricing. Either your project is the most luxurious or it's the budget alternative in the market. If a project competes on both amenities and pricing, the result is that the project will lose money. So it is your choice to base your marketing plan on featuring amenities or price, but as I mentioned before, try to be flexible in your choice so if market conditions or data change, you can change your marketing strategy.

> *"What everyone knows is what has already happened or become obvious. What the aware individual knows is what had not yet taken shape, what has not yet occurred."*
> —Sun Tzu, sixth century B.C.

Without question, marketability studies are more important than market research reports. I often recommend that after doing some basic market research (such as determining population, average household income, and demographics), you should stop your market research work and focus most of your efforts on the marketability study. Preparing a marketability study is your first step toward programming and designing your project. A marketability study is not easy to do. Market research, in comparison, is relatively easy to complete because market research is quantitative. The data can be obtained from any number of reliable and unreliable resources. A marketability study, on the other hand, forces you to prove that your project is viable from both the physical and the market aspects.

So, after doing some basic market research, focus on working to complete your marketability study. You may find as you work on the marketability study that you may have to do additional market research. That's fine, because you will not have wasted a lot of time gathering perhaps irrelevant data if you focus your time on preparing a market study.

It is very important to interpret the market data relative to your proposed project. Don't simply regurgitate market information.

The last part of a marketability study is to do a pricing analysis. The pricing analysis compares your proposed project with what you believe to be competitive projects. The pricing analysis is a basic appraisal analysis where if your project has amenities that your competition does not, you can then charge a higher price. On the other hand, if your project does not have amenities that your competition has, then you must reduce your price accordingly.

Through all of this, be prepared to change your idea or refine the data if necessary and as necessary—and do this as often as you need to do so. Keep in mind that at this stage of the development process, you have not bought a site and you should not have spent much, if any, money. You have complete flexibility at this point in the development process to change your proposed project or even your project concept to match any new information or changes in the market.

As I said earlier, the preparation of a marketability study is difficult. It takes time. Don't make the mistake of many, who focus on market research simply because it is relatively easy to do and avoid preparing a marketability study—many developers do. As I mentioned earlier, the marketability study takes the place of what was commonly used, that is, a consumer demand survey.

IMPORTANCE OF MARKETABILITY STUDIES REVISITED

Market and marketability studies are important because in one respect they stimulate and manage demand. The studies often stimulate demand because the target market is asked to consider needs and wants that perhaps the target market has never considered before. In this process, you will be able to manage the demand by asking specific and direct questions of your targeted market. This effort in essence creates new demand by making end users aware of their new needs and wants. In creating this new demand, you are to a certain extent practicing some of the principles of the *Blue Ocean Strategy*.

One common way to create new demand is to create dissatisfaction with old products that perhaps may be outdated in the face of new technology or new amenities. Consider this example: Most people use laundry detergent in their homes. It's been shown that people are very brand loyal when it comes to laundry detergent. Let's say that you have run out of your favorite laundry detergent. You have been using it for years and are very familiar with not only its name but also its package shape and color. You now go to the grocery store to purchase more laundry detergent; however, you cannot seem to find your laundry detergent package. You look around and eventually see that your brand of laundry detergent is now in a new shape of package and the package is a different color. Emblazoned on the label are three almost omnipresent words: "New and Improved." Did you know that you needed new and improved laundry detergent? Were you not happy with your laundry detergent the way it was? This is a simple but direct example of creating dissatisfaction with old products. It is an approach used by consumer product companies, and it is used by real estate developers as well.

> *"Success in business requires training and discipline and hard work. But, if you're not frightened by these things, the opportunities today are as great as they ever were."*
>
> —David Rockefeller

Finally, marketability studies are important because as you work through the process, you will identify the level, timing, and composition of the product (your proposed project). The information that you obtain in this process will often help you decide whether you should pursue a project today or at some point in the future. It will also help you with some basic information, such as what property type you should build.

IDEA REFINEMENT AND THE APPLICATION OF THE MARKETABILITY STUDY

As you refine your idea, you are studying it in specific physical detail, with the site and use identified (simply a marketability study). One of the easiest ways to accomplish this is to work with your prospective end users—investors and/or buyers—to develop a tentative program and schematic design for your proposed project. In short, you can often save yourself a lot of time by working with your constituencies, because they are the ones who will decide whether they will buy or lease your project, invest in your project, or give legal approval (entitlements) so that you can build your project. In short, you may have some phenomenal ideas for building a unique project. However, what really matters is what your constituencies think. What you think is irrelevant. It is your constituencies, and specifically your end users, who will buy or lease your project and should have their needs and wants satisfied. I often refer to this approach through a metaphor of gathering your jigsaw puzzle pieces. Your jigsaw puzzle pieces are the needs and wants of your constituencies. It's up to you to put these jigsaw puzzle pieces together in such a way that you have a completed picture or project.

THE PROCESS OF IDEA REFINEMENT

As you refine your idea, there is a distinct process that you will follow.

- Idea conception.
- Back-of-the-envelope analysis.
- Highest and best use analysis.
- Market studies.
- Financial feasibility analysis.

Let's look at each of these stages.

Formulating an idea often involves asking several questions. What does the developer imagine doing on this site? Who will use the space developed by the new project? How will the proposed project be integrated into its surrounding neighborhood? How might the project be financed? Answering these questions starts the feasibility study process. If you reflect back to the first chapter, and look closely at each of these four questions, you will recognize that these four questions are in essence the questions asked by the enterprise concept.

> *"The brave act quickly, while the timid drag their feet."*
>   —Sun Tzu, sixth century B.C.

Continuing, you need to get a bright idea! How does one get a bright idea? Well, you look at market signals, the market signals that perhaps you identified when doing your market research and preparing your preliminary draft of your marketability study. Often, bright ideas come from your experience. You have seen what has happened in certain communities that have similar characteristics, or you have read case studies that indicate characteristics like the site you are considering. Oftentimes, bright ideas come from dead sites or brownfield sites. The dead sites or brownfield sites can be relatively expensive; however, the cities are very interested in working with you as a developer to reclaim these dead or brownfield sites into productive tax-paying assets.

Next, begin to prepare a back-of-the-envelope analysis. Start with your idea, use your existing market information, and prepare a quick financial feasibility analysis. Developers often prepare a back-of-the-envelope analysis to make a very quick and fairly accurate initial decision about whether to further pursue a particular project on a particular site. Nevertheless, after completing a back-of-the-envelope analysis, you need to decide whether this proposed project meets your investment parameters. One of the most common investment parameters is to compare the results of your back-of-the-envelope analysis with your hurdle rate.

Although in this chapter we are talking about market and marketability studies, I want to go on a tangent and discuss hurdle rates. What exactly is a hurdle rate? A hurdle rate is commonly defined as the minimum acceptable investment rate. That said, if the return from the back-of-the-envelope analysis exceeds your hurdle rate, then you should proceed with the project to the next step. How do you calculate a hurdle rate? In business school, a hurdle rate is often defined as the weighted average cost of capital (WACC) and, more precisely, the marginal WACC. If we focus on this definition for a bit, we realize that if a hurdle rate is defined as the marginal WACC, then as the proposed project equals the hurdle rate, it is in essence a project that achieves breakeven. I suspect we are not in business simply to break even. So with that thought in mind, there are three things that should be added to the basic hurdle rate calculation.

1. Opportunity cost.
2. Risk.
3. Profit.

Let's look at each of these items. Opportunity cost says that by investing in one item, you cannot invest in another item given limited capital. As such, you may consider that by making such a decision to invest in one item, you are giving up return or have a cost associated with that decision. When I mention risk in this context, I am speaking of specific property-type or geographic risk. For example, many people think that investing in hotel properties is far riskier than investing in, say, office buildings. Thus, a risk premium should be added to this calculation if you are considering investing in a hotel project. Last is profit; how much profit you wish to make? If you consider adding these three items (opportunity cost, risk, and profit) to WACC, you have in essence calculated what I call a usable hurdle rate. With a usable hurdler rate as the minimum acceptable investment rate, any project that you invest in that exceeds your usable hurdle rate is guaranteed to cover your capital cost, risk, and opportunity cost and produce a profit. (Note: Some argue that opportunity cost, risk, and profit are already included in WACC. This is true, but it is the opportunity cost, risk, and profit of the provider of capital, not your opportunity cost, risk, and profit. A usable hurdle rate reflects your opportunity cost, risk, and profit.)

> *"As a rule in military operations, you need to change tactics a hundred times at every pace."*
>
> —Sun Tzu, sixth century B.C.

The WACC, opportunity cost, risk, and profit are personal to each of us. That is, we each have a different cost, we each have different things we can invest in that perhaps another cannot, we each have a different perspective of risk, and we each have a view on how much profit we would like to make.

Getting back on track, we now have to prepare a highest and best use analysis. You now have chosen the site, and now you need to seek the best use, or really the most fitting or the most probable use. The highest and best use essentially says it is the best financial use over time or the use that makes the most money. Understand that the highest and best use is often defined by you the developer, based on the pragmatic approach to development. In this stage, you choose what you think is the appropriate property type, its size, and its composition.

Last, you have to be cynical. You have a bright idea, but you have to ask yourself, Why me? Why has no other developer stumbled on this idea that I have? Is there anything wrong with my idea? Why exactly do I see an opportunity while others have not? These self-critical or cynical questions are extremely important to ensure that you do not make a mistake because of a lack of information or because you have just simply not learned of certain significant information that the rest of the market is aware of. So how exactly would you go about trying to find this information? You might visit the community and ask the citizens why a particular site has not been developed in the past. For example, if a site has been for sale for a number of years, ask why, exactly, the site has not been sold. If you go through this analysis of asking people and being self-critical, and you do not find any information that compromises your bright idea, then by all means move forward with your bright idea.

A bright idea, to be successful, should be developed around a total marketing concept and plan. You should be systematic in this approach by doing extensive market research and testing your ideas, responding to the needs and wants of your target market (the essence of a marketability

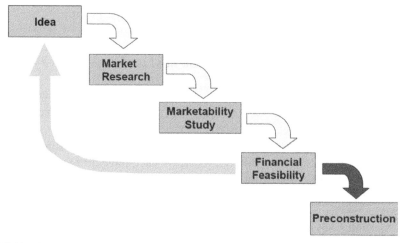

FIGURE 6.1 Development and Marketability Studies: An Iterative Process

study), identifying and recognizing your competition, and positioning and programming your project accordingly. The idea-refinement process is an iterative process. It follows the six-phase development process by first starting with your idea, testing your idea by doing some market research, proving your idea by doing a marketability study, and preparing a financial feasibility study. If you find, say, after preparing your financial feasibility study, that the return calculations do not meet your hurdle rates, then you must start at the beginning by changing or refining your idea and going through the process again. You should go through the idea refinement process as many times as you need to until your idea is supported by market research, which is in turn supported by your marketability study, which is then supported by your financial feasibility analysis. Once all aspects of this process are satisfactory to you, then, and only then, should you move on to the preconstruction phase (shown in Figure 6.1).

LEARNING POINTS FROM THIS CHAPTER

After reading this chapter, I should:

- Understand the components of marketability studies and why marketability studies are more important than market studies.
- Understand that an idea should be changed or refined as often as necessary at this stage.
- Know what a usable hurdle rate is and how it is calculated.

CHAPTER 7

Land Acquisition and Control

Before we talk about land acquisition and control, let's talk about site evaluation and selection. The first step of site selection is to determine what constitutes the cost-appropriate use for property. What is meant by the cost-appropriate use? In short, the most effective way of selecting a site is by evaluating the actual purchase price or cost relative to the cost and return of your proposed project. When considering the cost of a site or property, you work your financial analysis backwards, that is, determine the land or property cost that is most appropriate for your budget or development plan. You might have an initial idea of what you would like to build. With that in mind, determine the construction and development costs, determine the operating revenues and operating expenses, and incorporate the return target or hurdle rate. Then mathematically work backwards to determine the cost of the property, given what you would like to build and the hurdle rate. By using this approach, you determine the property purchase price that fits your needs. When you consider the purchase price of property, or its value, it's only worth what it's worth to you. Many developers get into financial or budget difficulties because they overpay for a property. You must realize that once you purchase the property, the cost is fixed. If, when doing a financial pro forma, a developer finds that the returns are not being met, the developer is forced to downsize or rescale the overall project programming. So, by working backwards mathematically, you determine the purchase price of the land or property that fits your needs or the cost-appropriate use.

Another aspect to consider when selecting a site is the location and rent aspects. The ultimate value of a project depends on where the property is located and how a proposed building or existing structure is situated on the site. The ultimate value is often dependent on things like visibility and access. For example, in Manhattan, buildings located with an avenue address are often valued more than buildings located with a street address.

Granted, the differences and value are often perception, but they could be based in reality. Say, for example, you would like to locate a retail business in Manhattan. An avenue address would be far more useful and valuable because avenues tend to have more traffic flow than streets. If you are considering, say, a retail site, where the existing or planned building is situated will determine the rent paid by tenants. For example, if a tenant space is located toward the front of the building, which has exterior windows and a high traffic count, the visibility is valued by the retailer, and thus the retailer is typically willing to pay more rent than for a tenant space located at the back of the retail space facing a brick wall or an alley. So it is essential to consider the location and rent aspects of a property you are surveying because the location and rent aspects will determine the ultimate value of your development project.

A useful method when you are trying to select a site is to create a list of features for different property types that you consider important for a site. If you are thinking about an office building with large service tenants, such as law firms and accounting firms, you will probably want to select a site for your proposed office building that has numerous linkages so that clients of your tenants can easily get to the building. If you are thinking about building a resort hotel property, you are likely to refine your search to physical sites that exceed 50 or 100 acres. Putting together this list of particular characteristics given a certain property type will help you narrow your focus and spend less time in selecting sites. If you plan to use a broker to help you in your search for a development property, brokers find these lists of characteristics very useful.

It's often said that when looking for an urban infill site, a developer might find a site that is looking for a use. What does this mean? Well, let's say you are walking through a city and notice an abandoned or semiabandoned building. Surrounding this building are several fully occupied residential buildings. As you walk around the area, you notice that there seem to be very few, if any, restaurants or grocery stores. Perhaps this abandoned or semiabandoned building might be a superb site for a grocery store or a restaurant. In short, this is a site looking for a use. Sometimes when a site is looking for a use, you do not or should not change its use. Since this hypothetical abandoned or semiabandoned building is surrounded by fully occupied residential buildings, you should consider why the building is not occupied. Perhaps the reason is that the building you're looking at is simply an older, out-of-date building that is in need of renovation. The idea of a site looking for a use is directly addressed by the enterprise concept, where the enterprise concept asks what the most probable and best-fitting use is.

NONSPATIAL AND SPATIAL MARKETS

An important concept to understand when you select a site is the difference between nonspatial and spatial markets. Nonspatial markets are ambiguous. An example of a nonspatial market might be the United States. Consider, how would you market to the whole of the United States? Yes, the United States is a market, but there are too many separate markets, and it must be broken down. Similarly, how would you market to Pennsylvania? Again, too broad of a market. How about the Chestnut Hill area of Philadelphia? Now we are starting to consider a smaller segment of the broad market, or a spatial market. A spatial market starts with your defined target market and then includes the unique project that you plan to build and all of its amenities and features.

You create a spatial monopoly by considering linkages, visibility, demand generators, amenities, and the like. In theory, if you have determined that your target market has the sole need and want of being in a brand-new building, then, when you build a brand-new building—for that moment— you have a spatial monopoly. However, creating a spatial monopoly by itself is not enough. You must *maintain* a spatial monopoly. How do you maintain a spatial monopoly? By continuous market research of your competition. As I've mentioned before, market research is a perpetual functional activity of the developer. Just as you will locate and analyze your competition to determine what they have or do not have as part of their building, each of your competitors will be looking at you and your building to determine what amenities you have or don't have.

> *"It's so damned much fun [development] that it gets to be a habit—so you wind me up and I build a hotel."*
> —Steve Wynn, chairman and CEO of Wynn Resorts Ltd.,
> Bloomberg Business News, January 30, 2003

Maintaining a spatial monopoly is essential. Consider the generic definition of a monopoly. A monopoly is the sole source of a particular product or service in a market and thus can garner the highest price in that market. If a particular product—or, in our case, building—garners the highest price in the market, that means that our building has the highest value in the market for our target market. If a particular building loses its monopoly, it becomes a commodity. A commodity is average and has average pricing. It does not serve our purpose to develop a building that is going to compete as a commodity. Since our ultimate goal as a developer is to create value, maintaining a spatial monopoly again is essential.

ELEMENTS OF DESIGN

I mentioned earlier in this chapter that it would be helpful to put together a list of characteristics for site selection. Let's say that we are now considering specific sites. Again, it is useful to put together a list of characteristics of the specific sites to help us in deciding which site we should eventually purchase. A good outline for doing this is called the *elements of design,* which breaks down the characteristics of a site into five categories or subsets:

1. Physical attributes (static).
2. Legal/political attributes.
3. Linkage attributes.
4. Dynamic attributes.
5. Environmental attributes.

You will use the elements of design in two situations in the development process. The first situation is now, when you are trying to select a site to acquire. The second time will be when you are programming and designing the project.

Let's define each of the subsets. Before we do, I want to explain that by putting together the elements of design, you are not making a decision; you are simply cataloging or compiling information.

Let's consider the physical attributes. In essence, you are cataloging the physical attributes of the site you are considering, such as the dimensions, physiography, hydrology, habitat, easements, physical improvements, and historical characteristics. (Historical characteristics in this instance could be official or unofficial. If the site is officially a historical site, it is obvious; typically it has a plaque prominently placed on the site. But part of the work in determining the physical attributes should be a search of the historical records of the site, such as identifying the previous owners of the site and the prior use of the site.) By cataloging the physical attributes of the site, you are trying to identify any potential situations or attributes that may affect your decision to purchase a particular site.

When cataloging the legal and political attributes of the site, you are trying to understand the zoning conditions and possible special zoning options, existing or pending litigation, building codes, public controls, and the like. This information is relatively easy to obtain because it is public information and can be obtained by going to the city planning or building department and simply asking for the information.

When cataloging the linkage attributes, you are trying to identify the traditional linkages, such as streets, sidewalks, rail stations, and public transit access, but in this situation you are also trying to determine the utility services to the site. If your site is in a rural location, you might have to bring utility service (water, sewer, electricity) to the site. This entails additional cost, of course, but again at this time, you simply want to catalog information. If you are building in a city location, your site most likely has utility services; however, it is likely that you will have to increase the capacity of the utilities. This entails additional cost for your project, but again, you do not want to be making decisions at this time, just simply cataloging information.

The dynamic attributes of the site include things like the visual factors. What do you see when you look at the site or when you stand in the site and look outward? What are the prevailing air currents and possible airborne pollution? Does the site have any historical community reputation or values? A site might not have any official historical significance yet have significance to the local community because it was often used for, say, a street fair or a circus. You might also consider what you see as you approach the site—what is called the approach zone. The approach zone can range from a distance of a few feet to several miles. What you see as you move through the approach zone to a particular site directly affects the impression you have of the site. For example, if you have to pass a junkyard and some abandoned buildings before you come upon a site, your impression of the site— even if it has a new luxury building—is diminished. You might note as part of the dynamic attributes that you might have to condition the image of the approach zone. Image-conditioning the approach zone means that you will work closely with the city to clean up or beautify the route leading toward your site by cleaning up the trash, adding new landscaping features, or adding or updating street lights, for example.

Last, you need to catalog the environmental attributes. The environmental attributes are factors such as the social impact and objectives of your project, the fiscal impact and objectives of your project, and the ethical factors and objectives. Most of the adversarial depictions of the city-developer relationship exist in this last category, environmental attributes. For example, a city is very concerned about how a new building will affect the community, as is the community itself. But if you reflect for a moment, the government, the community, and the developer have the same objectives with regard to the social impact of the project, that is, to improve the place in which people live, work, and play. Similarly, the government is very interested in the fiscal or financial impact of the project, as is the community. The government should realize increased tax revenues with a new or renovated building, and the community should realize lower taxes as a result of increased commercial tax revenue. Needless to say, the developer is looking forward to collecting a developer fee and earning a reversionary profit upon completion of the project. Given what was just stated, it is difficult to understand why a government, community, and developer are depicted as having adversarial relationships when you consider that the government, community, and the developer are all trying to achieve the same things as far as the social and fiscal impacts of a project, that is, to increase revenue or save money and to improve the place where people live, work, and play.

TARGET MARKETS AND MARKET SHARE

As you search for a site and complete the elements of design, part of the effort is to determine the initial market area boundaries for your project. In that regard, there are three things that your project must have to be successful: attraction, draw, and critical mass. Let's consider a retail project (Figure 7.1) that is located across railroad tracks from a house. To get to this retail project, the resident must travel, in this example, 1½ miles to reach the track crossing and then 1½ miles to the retail center. Let's say the resident wants to go to a dry cleaner. If another retail center that has a dry

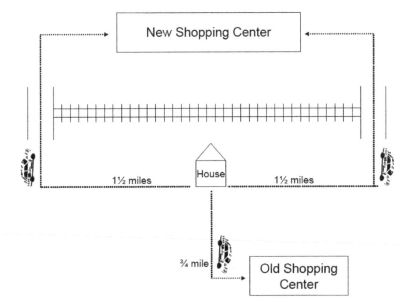

FIGURE 7.1 Example of Project Attraction, Draw, and Critical Mass

cleaner is on the same side of the railroad tracks as the resident and only three-quarters of a mile away, it is very unlikely that the resident will travel three miles one way (six miles round trip) just to go to a dry cleaner. So the developer of the retail project on the other side of the tracks must design a project that has an attraction for the resident. Perhaps the attraction is a unique store that does not exist elsewhere in the area. A developer has to identify and consider the competitive influence of nearby projects and possible physical barriers.

Expanding on this attraction as the draw for the residents are stores that residents find desirable leading to the retail project and having a critical mass. An example might be an IKEA store in a retail center. IKEA stores are generally spaced far apart, but because IKEA stores have a broad range of products desired by many people in one location, they fit the characteristics of having attraction, draw, and critical mass. The key goal of the developer is to create and maintain a spatial monopoly for the project. By creating and maintaining a spatial monopoly for the project, the developer creates attraction, draw, and critical mass to bring in the target market.

You will be relying on the market external demand and leakage. External demand is simply market demand from outside the primary market area (Figure 7.2). External demand often occurs when a building has a spatial monopoly and no competition. Eventually a market grows, and market leakage occurs as a competitor takes another building's primary target market (Figure 7.3). The reality is that today's developer hopes to utilize market leakage for a project. This idea ties directly into the definition of a spatial monopoly, which is why maintaining a spatial monopoly is so important.

As you consider market conditions and your potential target market, you will try to seek a site with a cost-appropriate use that is needed and

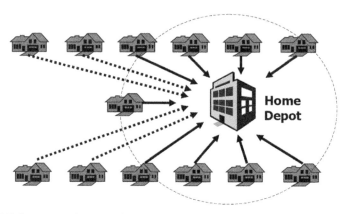

FIGURE 7.2 External Demand

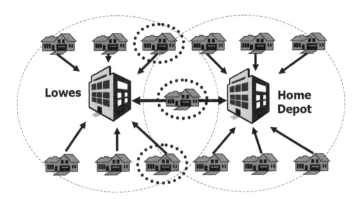

FIGURE 7.3   Market Leakage

wanted by your potential target market. Finding an appropriate use again is an iterative process, and as we mentioned before, you should classify the desired attributes for a site and a given project or property type. As you catalog the characteristics of several sites by using the elements of design, you should try to eliminate potential uses for which a site lacks essential criteria. When we were discussing how to devise an idea for a project, I suggested that you consider the negatives of the situation. Similarly, when trying to choose a site for development, you should review the elements of design and begin to eliminate sites to the point where you only have one, two, or perhaps three sites to choose from.

Remember that market areas are dynamic. Consider the information obtained by completing the elements of design, and reposition your idea by adjusting and/or conforming your project to the defined market by establishing a spatial monopoly.

SITE CONTROL AND ACQUISITION

The objective of site acquisition is control, not necessarily ownership—at least not yet. There are a number of ways to obtain control over a site:

- Purchase.
- Option.
- Joint venture with landowner.
- Ground lease.

Your situation might dictate that you have to purchase the property. On the other hand, given the appropriate market conditions, you might be able to obtain an option to purchase the property and in this way gain control over the site. These two points are discussed in detail shortly. Perhaps you have identified a site, but the landowner is not interested in selling the site to you. You might consider doing a joint venture with that landowner, where the land is contributed in exchange for an equity interest in your to-be-developed building. This is an interesting strategy because two things occur: The first is that you as developer can use the joint venture as a method of financing. Let's say that you convince the landowner to contribute land in exchange for a 50 percent interest in your to-be-developed building. The landowner receives a capital account for a 50 percent interest and you, in order to match his capital account, pay or contribute monies for only 50 percent of the land value. There are a number of ways to do this, but this is the simplest. This is an interesting strategy for a developer because the landowner has visions of the value of the 50 percent ownership interest. The reality is that the landowner may never receive any return from the project if, for example, the project is not successful. You, on the other hand, as developer obtain control of the site by only having to finance 50 percent of the costs of the property.

Another method of obtaining control over property is to arrange a ground lease with the landowner. In my view, arranging a ground lease from the landowner is one of the most underutilized methods of gaining control over property. A ground lease offers a developer a major advantage that is directly tied to the actual costs and reflects it in a development budget. A developer who actually purchases property has to place the acquisition cost in the budget. A development budget may show that costs are too high and perhaps investor returns are too low. With a ground lease, you as developer could put only the ground lease payments during the development in the budget. As a result, your development costs will be lower (as opposed to acquiring property), and thus the investor returns will be higher. Using a ground lease, given the strategy outlined earlier, often can make a development project proceed. A ground lease also has several advantages for the property owner. One distinct advantage is tax savings. Under U.S. tax law, if the property owner preferred to accept the full purchase price of the land, the property owner would have to pay capital gains tax on the profit at that time. If the property owner arranges a ground lease with the developer, the property owner only pays ordinary taxes on the ground lease payments actually received. Often, a property owner is not interested in selling a property at this time. One reason that can be inferred from this paragraph is that the property owner's tax basis may be very low relative to today's market value or sales price. As a result, the profit on the sale would be very large, and thus the tax would be very high. Some property owners are not interested in selling their property because they would like to keep the property in the family for future generations. A ground lease accomplishes this goal. A ground lease through its ground lease payments provides an annuity for future generations of the property owner's family.

Now, let us discuss the use of options to acquire control over property. A *caveat:* Property or real estate law in the United States is governed by the state in which the property is located. The laws are similar among the states, but they are different. My comments address the common practices in most states. I strongly advise you to seek the counsel of an attorney experienced in the state where you plan to develop property.

Options are a good way for you the developer to acquire control of property. An option allows you, the optionee, to call upon the property owner, the optionor, to sell the property to you. An option may be exercised at any time during the option or upon the occurrence of certain events. A key point to understand about options: When an option agreement is signed between the optionee and the optionor, the option agreement is binding only on the optionor. The optionee has no obligation to exercise the option to purchase the property. For this reason alone, you can understand why an option agreement is so valuable to the developer. It provides flexibility. If you decide as a developer, for whatever reason, to not acquire the property, you do not have to. You can walk away from the option agreement for any reason; frankly, in most cases you do not have to give a reason.

For this last reason, the optionor often puts conditions into the option agreement to ensure that the optionee simply does not walk away from the option contract. The common reason for an option agreement is so that the optionee, the developer, has a due diligence period to investigate the property (soil tests, environmental tests, zoning variances, etc.). An experienced optionor puts conditions into an option agreement that state, for example, if a soil test to be performed is successful, then the option would be exercised by the optionee automatically.

A mistake that's often made by an inexperienced optionee (developer) is not understanding what happens when an optionee exercises the option. For an option agreement to be legally valid, the option agreement simply has to consist of an offer, acceptance, and consideration. The option agreement should specify the names of the optionee and optionor, property description, purchase price, time of the option, and option payments (if any). In theory, a legally binding option agreement could be one page long. When an optionee exercises an option, the option agreement novates (changes) into a purchase and sale agreement. Thus, an option agreement should contain all the representations, warranties, conditions, and covenants that you want in a purchase and sale agreement. In many situations, optionees have not included all the representations, warranties, conditions, and covenants that they would want in a typical purchase and sale agreement. The representations, warranties, conditions, and covenants can be included in the option agreement itself, or a purchase and sale agreement can be attached to the option agreement as an exhibit. Which method is used is a matter of style that is often dictated by the attorney you use. The option agreement, in essence, establishes a due diligence period when you can validate and verify the representations, warranties, conditions, and covenants in the option agreement.

So when you are negotiating an option agreement, everything is fully negotiable—at a price. Like any contract, what is desired by either party often adjusts the price (purchase price of the property and/or option price). What is typically considered in an option price? Generally speaking, the option price is based on two things: (1) opportunity cost and (2) sharing costs. None of this is written anywhere, but it's understood that these two things are the basis of the option price. An optionor who gives an option on a property will be restricted from selling the property to anyone else during the option period. So, after agreeing to a sales price in the option agreement, the optionor takes a risk of the market conditions changing unfavorably. For example, if market conditions change such that the market value of the property increases, then the optionor in effect loses money for having already agreed to a purchase price that is less than the current market value. The situation is clearly an opportunity cost on the part of the optionor. If, for example, market conditions change such that the market value of the property decreases, the optionor is still obligated under the option agreement, while the optionee can walk away at any time, which is likely. But the optionor cannot terminate the option agreement until the optionee states that she or he will not exercise the option or until the option period expires. On the other hand, given the first circumstance of market value increasing beyond the stated purchase price, the optionee is in the favorable situation of having already locked in a purchase price for the property, even though the market value has increased above that purchase price.

During the option period, the optionee typically covers the carrying costs of the optionor's property. The carrying costs might include property taxes, insurance, and operating expenses (if applicable). Again, these two points—opportunity cost and carrying costs—are not written down anywhere, but it's expected that the optionee would pay for these costs through the option payment. The option price in essence is what can be negotiated in the current market. It could be a dollar, or it could be virtually the purchase price of the property.

One practical recommendation is that you, the developer, should always be the one to offer an option agreement to a property owner. If a property owner offers an option agreement to you as a potential purchaser, you should be very suspicious. The property owner in this situation probably cannot sell the property and therefore offers option agreements and collects the option payment, perhaps knowing clearly that the optionee will not exercise the option because of some defect in the property. The property owner collects the option payment, puts the option payment in the bank, and then seeks another person who is willing to execute an option agreement.

When you consider whether to use a sale and purchase agreement or an option agreement, several things have to be considered. First of all, you will probably not be able to get an option agreement on every property you pursue. An option agreement is typically only available in tight market situations. If there is a vibrant market, there is no incentive for a property owner to offer an option agreement instead of simply selling the property directly. But what is the difference between a sale and purchase agreement and an option agreement? Both agreements specify the property and the purchase price, among other things, and both agreements establish a due diligence period. The essential difference between the two agreements is how much flexibility you have as the buyer or optionee. With an option agreement, you essentially have the right as an optionee to walk away from the option agreement for any reason or no reason at all. With a purchase and sale agreement, your objections have to be stated and have to be material. Once your objections are given to the property seller, the property seller has the right to cure. What can the property seller typically do to cure your objection? The property seller can resolve your objection or can adjust the purchase price. If you discover while doing a phase 1 environmental study that the property is contaminated, the property seller can either remediate the contamination or reduce the purchase price to essentially cover the costs of remediation. Needless to say, the credit at closing to reduce the purchase price to cover the costs of remediation may not be sufficient, in your opinion. Perhaps the contamination is of a particularly difficult type, and you and the property seller become involved in a heated negotiation. In theory, the property seller could reduce the purchase price to a dollar in curing your objection, and you would be obligated to purchase the property. So the thought given this situation is to be sure that when negotiating either a contract for purchase and sale or an option agreement, you should specify the remedies, given certain circumstances, in the actual agreements so there is no confusion. In both purchase and sale agreement and option agreement situations, you are trying to control your risk during property acquisition. You attempt to control the risk by including comprehensive contingency clauses and warranties, thoroughly researching public records for past uses and potential problems, and premarketing your development concept to the community. Regarding this last point, if while premarketing your development concept to the community, there is a lot of opposition or NIMBYism, you may decide that this is not the appropriate site to acquire.

As you negotiate and read through purchase and sale or option agreements, you should be very familiar with legal definitions and concepts. It is outside the scope of this book, let alone this chapter, to go through a variety of legal definitions and concepts, although several of the most important are discussed in the glossary to this book. You should either acquire a legal terminology dictionary or take a basic business law course to familiarize yourself with this terminology.

Now that you've decided to actually purchase a specific site, you have to decide on the appropriate ownership structure for purchasing the property. Ownership structures range from sole ownership to partnerships to limited liability companies and C corporations. Again, which ownership structure you choose for purchasing property should be decided between you and your attorney. While you may predominantly use a particular type of ownership structure in your business, there is no one perfect structure to use. The decision to choose a particular type of ownership structure is usually based upon three things:

1. Control: the control you wish to have over the ownership entity.
2. Liability: the amount of liability you are willing to accept.
3. Taxes: what level of taxes you will be paying because of the ownership entity you've chosen.

PUBLIC AND PRIVATE RESTRICTIONS ON LAND USE

There are numerous public restrictions on an owner's ability to use real property. The most common is zoning. Zoning restrictions restrict how both private and business landowners may use their property. Courts consistently require zoning regulations to be limited in their focus to specific areas, such as health, safety, and general welfare—the basic reasoning for governments having police powers. When a zoning rule goes beyond health, safety, and general welfare, courts may strike down the zoning regulation as excessive, too broad, or overreaching. This last point is often used by developers attempting to seek zoning variances in a community. But it is a difficult argument to make and have prevail.

On the other hand, developers often prevail in arguments over aesthetic zoning regulations. Aesthetic zoning is a regulation that requires all architecture (materials, colors, sizes, etc.) to meet specified standards. Cities and towns enact aesthetic zoning ordinances to maintain (or preserve) a general overall appearance for structures in the community.

Zoning ordinances come in three broad categories: residential, commercial, and industrial. Residential zoning ordinances, which vary from city to city, often include single-family residences, townhouses, multifamily, assisted living, and student housing (college dormitories).

Commercial zoning ordinances can cover a number of different property types. Industrial zoning ordinances can include light, medium, and heavy industry, with appropriate governing regulations. The industrial zoning ordinances often address placement of structures in relation to residential areas, as well as limiting the types of chemical effects and processes that can be used on a site.

Zoning ordinances are not always rigid. There are exceptions for property types that may continue to be used in their current state, even though the property types do not currently conform to zoning ordinances and regulations. These exceptions include:

- Nonconforming use.
- Conditional use permit.
- Variance.

Nonconforming use is a classification that is reserved for a property structure that predates the enactment of the current zoning regulation. An example of a nonconforming use might be an older single-family home in an area that has transitioned to commercial uses.

A conditional use permit allows a business entity to operate in an area that has been reserved for residential use. A conditional use permit allows the property to be used in a way that is not in strict compliance with the zoning classification but does provide the business an essential service. An example is an attorney who works from home and meets clients there from time to time.

Zoning boards issue variances to allow a degree of flexibility in zoning regulations to recognize that zoning regulations cannot limit use entirely. An example might be a variance for heights, setback, or exterior façade. A developer of commercial property frequently gets involved with seeking variances of zoning ordinances for a proposed project. These variances could be minor or could be quite major. Later in the book, we talk about public-private partnerships, which can make the process of seeking a zoning variance significantly easier.

Believe it or not, there can be unconstitutional or illegal zoning regulations when, say, zoning ordinances are used to discriminate against members of society or are against public policy. The situation does not happen often, but it does come up from time to time, particularly in smaller towns.

> *"To be effective in real property involvements, one must simultaneously be, and provide the perspective of, historian, behaviorist, global citizen, urban planner, geographer, business strategist, futurist, political economist, accountant, researcher and information specialist."*
> —Stephen Roulac, president, Roulac Real Estate Consulting Group, in *Pyramid Power*, a publication of Pyramid Realty Group, June 18, 2004

There is also a concept known as spot zoning. Spot zoning is used by zoning boards to single out any particular parcel for special treatment. An example might be a developer who is allowed to build a mixed-use project, including a residential component, on a parcel that is covered by commercial zoning regulations. While the mixed-use project clearly has commercial components, perhaps the specific commercial zoning regulation does not allow for a residential component. Spot zoning would allow a developer in agreement with the town to include a residential component.

Building codes are local or state rules and regulations that have specific restrictions on the way that buildings can be constructed. Examples might include how the heating and air-conditioning systems are installed or how plumbing and electrical work is completed.

Planning boards are responsible for trying to manage property development in the community. They work in conjunction with the town's building department to create zoning regulations that do not conflict with building codes, and vice versa.

A unique type of public restriction on land use is a historical district designation. When a particular area is designated as such, it receives special protection on both state and local levels. The historical designation could encompass an entire building, both exterior and interior, it could just include the façade, or it could cover an area of the town. If a property has a historical designation, what a developer can and cannot do to the building is restricted. However, a historical designation could enable a developer to qualify for historical tax credits and thus reduce the overall cost for the project.

In addition to public restrictions on land use, there are also private restrictions, such as restrictive covenants or deed restrictions. A property owner can create a series of covenants and record them, put them in a deed, or record a plat (subdivision plan) that contains the restrictive covenants; then any subsequent owner takes the property subject to these limitations. A restrictive covenant, or deed restriction, is in essence a contract.

Restrictive covenants remain with the land parcel and are not specific to the owners. So, once created, restrictive covenants apply to all future owners. Typical restrictive covenants include:

- Establishing minimum lot sizes.
- Limiting the use of a parcel (such as residential use only).
- Limiting the number of outbuildings on a parcel.
- Restricting the types of animals that can live on the premises, such as forbidding farm animals.
- Requiring that all buildings conform to a general architectural theme.
- Forbidding certain types of activities on a parcel (such as selling alcohol).

Restrictive covenants are a private contract. As such, they must be enforced through civil lawsuits by those affected by such restrictive covenants. They cannot be enforced through public actions, such as the police.

Like illegal zoning ordinances, there can't be illegal or unconstitutional restrictive covenants. Restrictive covenants, for example, cannot be used to prevent people of a certain race, religion, or national origin from owning property in specific neighborhoods, and they cannot be against public policy.

Restrictive covenants can be removed only by the owner who originally placed the covenant. But there are exceptions. If you recall, a restrictive covenant is a contract. As a contract, a number of conditions can be placed within the restrictive covenant; for example, a restrictive covenant could expire after a certain period of time. One of the rare times that the public, through the courts, can remove a restrictive covenant is when it becomes illegal or against public policy. An example of this occurred in the southern part of the United States, where when slavery was still considered legal, property owners on occasion put restrictive covenants on their property to prevent blacks from owning their property.

LEARNING POINTS FROM THIS CHAPTER

After reading this chapter, I should:

- Understand how a developer goes about selecting a site for development.
- Know the difference between nonspatial and spatial markets and the importance of a spatial market.
- Know the elements of design and how they are used.
- Understand the criteria for initially determining market area boundaries and how external demand and market leakage play a role.
- Know some of the methods for obtaining site control.
- Understand public and private restrictions on land use.

CHAPTER 8

Land Planning and Siting

I will not be getting into too much detail here about site design and layout because a thorough discussion is well beyond the scope of this book, but instead I will show you some pictures to identify some common considerations. One of the first site layout considerations is the allocation of space. As a developer, you will have to consider three common allocation issues: potential land contributions, green space, and roads. In many cases, a particular land parcel cannot be built on 100 percent of the parcel. The parcel may have wetlands, for example, or the city in which the parcel is located may require that a certain percentage of the land parcel be dedicated to green space or contributed for a public use such as a playground. If you are contemplating building, say, a single-family home development and a multiple-building multifamily complex or office complex, you'll have to subtract some of the land parcel area for roads and parking space. So, as you review a potential parcel for acquisition, you should consider these parcel allocation issues to determine the actual amount of buildable land on your land parcel (Figure 8.1). In addition to considering the horizontal plane of buildable land, you also have to consider the FAR (floor area ratio) requirements, which will define the amount of vertical buildable area.

VALUE CREATION

Let's look at site plans and try to understand why the site was laid out the way it was. In Figure 8.2, at the top to the left of the site is a Wal-Mart store. To the right below the Wal-Mart store is a strip of in-line stores. Adjacent to the site above the Wal-Mart store is a highway. Drivers on the highway have clear visibility of the Wal-Mart store. At the right of the site plan is a road by which customers can access the site. Any wonder why Wal-Mart is pushed to the back and in the corner of the site? It follows the principle of why a grocery store puts milk in the back of the store. Milk is

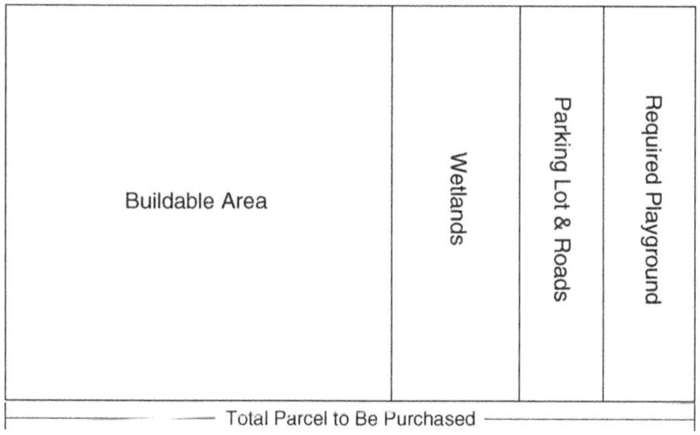

Buildable Area
Wetlands
Parking Lot & Roads
Required Playground
Total Parcel to Be Purchased

FIGURE 8.1 Parcel Space Allocation

State Highway 617
WAL★MART
FUTURE EXPANSION AREA
PHASE I
PHASE II
PAD B

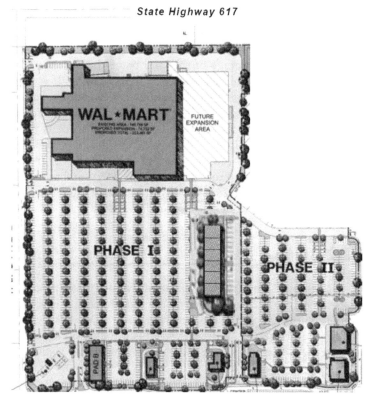

FIGURE 8.2 Site Layout Example

considered a staple, and customers who wish to purchase the milk have to pass by a variety of other groceries and perhaps be enticed to make an impulse purchase. In the same vein, customers have to pass by the strip stores before reaching the Wal-Mart store. The Wal-Mart store is the equivalent of milk for this retail site. As a result of these strip stores having a good amount of traffic flow past them, their rent will be higher than it otherwise would be, which creates additional value because of the higher rents for the entire retail center. At the bottom of the site are several rectangles representing buildings. These buildings are referred to as out-parcels or out-lots. Assuming that the remaining parking ratio still complies with the building code and zoning ordinances, these out-parcels or out-lots usually enhance the value of a retail center. Typically, they are occupied by banks or fast-food restaurants. One of two things can occur: The land for the out-parcel could be sold to a third-party retailer, who would then build its own store building there, or a developer could put up a building on the site and then lease the building to a retail tenant. Another alternative is that a developer could ground-lease the parcel to the retail tenant, who would then build a store on the site. Having an out-parcel on this site is important for increasing the value of the site and doing something that most people don't think about. Regarding the first point, if a developer sells or leases an out-parcel lot to a retailer, clearly the property's revenue stream is enhanced and thus the value is increased. But secondly, particularly by selling an out-parcel, the developer actually recoups part of this capital investment in the land, which would typically be accomplished only by selling the overall property.

> *"Without leaps of imagination, or dreaming, we lose the excitement of possibilities. Dreaming, after all, is a form of planning."*
> —Gloria Steinem

Figure 8.3 is another retail site. For this example, let's assume that this is a fully leased cash-flowing property, in other words, a grayfield site. Following the definition of a grayfield site, a developer purchases a grayfield site to increase its value; otherwise, there is no point in purchasing the site. Let's also assume that this particular site is for sale. So, as you look at Figure 8.3, what do you do to enhance the value of this retail site? (Keep in mind that we are only addressing site placement and not the condition or design of the buildings on the site.) There are two possibilities for enhancing the site. The first is putting up a building that attaches the two sets of buildings on the site (currently green space) perhaps placing an anchor store in this

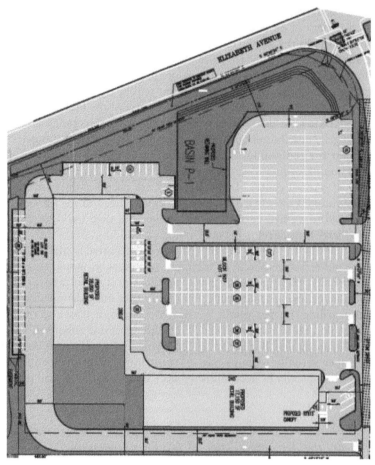

FIGURE 8.3 Another Site: Layout Example

new building. Also, a strip of stores could be built in the empty space on the right side or the top right area of the drawing. You must be careful, however, because one road extends along the right side of the site from top to bottom and along the top. You do not want to build strip stores that might visually block the stores that are already there.

In both Figure 8.2 and Figure 8.3, by placing certain buildings in certain locations, you've directly and positively affected the revenue stream and inevitably the value of the property. Hence, when you are considering a particular site or two, you must also consider how the buildings will be placed on the site, which will directly affect the value of your property.

PROJECT PROGRAMMING AND DESIGN

In a simplistic way, programming of a project is related to the planned use of a project. When programming a project, you consider what the property type should be, the site layout and design, and the tenant selection and tenant placement. The design of a project is related to its physical look, whether that means the style or the quality or type of materials. The style of a project could be traditional, modern, rustic, or various other possibilities. The quality of material could be high, with luxury materials such as marble and granite, or it could be unadorned poured-in-place concrete.

ELEMENTS OF DESIGN—AGAIN

Again, as you consider selecting a particular site for development, you should consider the specific aspects of the elements of design. The site topography, for example, will determine where you can place your buildings on the site. As you look at a particular site that you are considering purchasing, you have to complete the checklist of the elements of design as comprehensively as possible.

TALKING TO END USERS

Once again, active discussions with prospective tenants are incredibly valuable. Prospective tenants typically have a very defined notion of their proposed rental space. Prospective tenants may desire a location adjacent to, say, a busy road or away from a busy road. Prospective tenants may prefer one-story buildings, or they may prefer multiple stories. In particular, focus on specific, primary or lead tenants. Learn their criteria and desires, but more important, get their buy-in for the project by outlining the planned features of the proposed project. By gathering this valuable information of tenant needs and wants, you are helped with your site selection criteria. As you ask prospective tenants about their needs and wants for a proposed project, and you tell the prospective tenant that you can meet those needs and wants, you in essence are selling your space to that tenant. For example, if a prospective tenant wants a particular size of space and you can deliver it (among many other features), meeting the tenant's needs and wants, why wouldn't that prospective tenant sign a lease with you? I like to call the data obtained from prospective tenants jigsaw puzzle pieces. It is your job to put these jigsaw puzzle pieces together in such a way that you have a building that prospective tenants desire. As part of this inquiry process, you will find that you also obtain information about competitive projects. How does this happen? You may make a proposal to a prospective tenant who likes your ideas but then states that he met with another developer recently who gave a slightly different proposal. If you ask that prospective tenant to expand on the other developer's proposal, you are gathering some very important market data that you can use to enhance your proposed project. This market information is far, far more valuable than any information you would obtain from a database somewhere.

With all this in mind, how many tenants should be contacted, and what kinds of tenants should be contacted? The answer is actually very simple. You should contact tenants of all types, and you should contact as many tenants as you possibly can. You should not limit your contact with prospective tenants to those who might be interested in your current project or projects because as you speak to prospective tenants—or, in essence, as you network—you will get ideas about future projects that can be added to your development pipeline. A developer's pipeline is critically important because you will perhaps consider 10 or 20 projects before you find the first project that you would like to move forward with. A developer cannot focus solely on one project at a time, which ignores the fact that it takes time to find a viable project. When finished working on a single project, the developer then will spend time searching for new product but does not have a revenue stream from development fees.

TENANT MIX AND MARKETABILITY

We have been considering the importance of selecting a particular site and how to place buildings on a particular site, but we have so far overlooked one of the most important aspects of the development project, the tenants— who they are and where they are or would be located within the building. You need the right mix of tenants to achieve an overall synergism of the building, particularly a retail building. In a retail building, you need to consider the balance between national tenants, regional chains, and independent (including mom and pop) stores. By definition, national tenants will be a draw for your retail center that create traffic flow, but these tenants know about their importance in your retail center and often negotiate for some of the lowest rents. Thus, if you were to place all national tenants in your retail center, you would have a very low risk because of their typical financial status; however, rents will be low, and thus the value of the building will be low. On the other hand, if you filled your retail center with mom-and-pop stores, your risk for the stores would be very high, but your rents would be very high and thus the value of your building would be very high. So what you try to accomplish is a balance between national tenants, regional chains, and independent stores.

I often use two thoughts that describe what you are doing when working on the tenant mix and what you are trying to accomplish by balancing the types of tenants in your building. First: A building has no value. Although the physical bricks and mortar of a building have some residual value, the true value of a commercial property is in the leases. Second: A building is nothing more than a portfolio of leases, not unlike a portfolio of stocks. In your portfolio you have to consider concentration, diversification, risk, and yield. So by manipulating the balance of tenants within your building, you are directly affecting the concentration, diversification, risk, and yield of your portfolio of leases. "A building is nothing more than a portfolio of leases"

Now that you have decided on the mix of tenants for your building, you have to consider the tenant placement. Where tenants are located within the building is not a random exercise. Tenants are placed in the building with the hope that they'll contribute to the building and the value of that building. Tenant placement:

- Determines pricing.
- Establishes traffic flow.
- Creates competition and/or synergy.
- Promotes design or atmosphere.

As we saw in Figure 8.2, the in-line stores that had to be passed by customers before reaching the Wal-Mart store should pay more because of the traffic flow created by the Wal-Mart store. Similarly, if a retail store is placed near the front entrance of the building and thus has high visibility and obviously good traffic flow, that space should garner higher rent from a tenant than a space in the back of the building in a corner facing a brick wall.

In a retail building, you might like to have three shoe store tenants. By placing these three shoe stores next to each other, does that create synergy? Well, it might create synergy if the shoe stores catered to different clienteles, such as men, women, and children or at different price points for their shoes. If the shoe stores all sold women's shoes at the same price point, there might be strong competition among the tenants. Although tenants do not view it favorably, the competition might increase the overall sales and thus (percentage) rent to you, the developer, and thus increase the value of the retail center. And if you decide to place high-end tenants such as Bloomingdale's, Tiffany's, and Nordstrom's in your retail center, clearly the image or atmosphere of the retail center is high-end (as would the construction cost of the building on account of high-end finishes). If your tenants are a Dollar Store, a consignment store, and an outlet store, the image of the retail center would be low-end and have a lower construction cost.

> *"In Dallas, I can get a developmental approval in nine months. Around San Francisco or Los Angeles, it can take a decade—lawsuits included."*
>
> —A developer quoted on zoning nightmares in Business 2.0 Magazine, November 2005

Let us consider some examples of good and bad tenant placement within a retail center. In Figure 8.4, you see a very common style of retail strip center. Let's say that you would like to have a Weight Watchers store next to a Godiva chocolate store. Is this good tenant placement? Does this placement of the two tenants create competition or synergy? Do the tenants create traffic flow for each other? Think about the answers to these

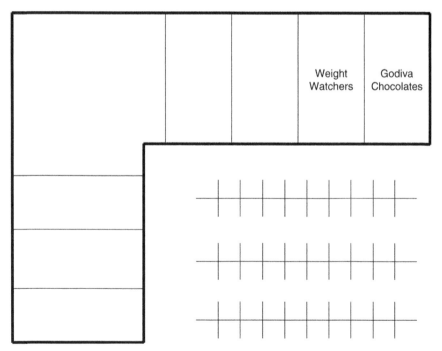

FIGURE 8.4 Good and Bad Tenant Placement: Example 1

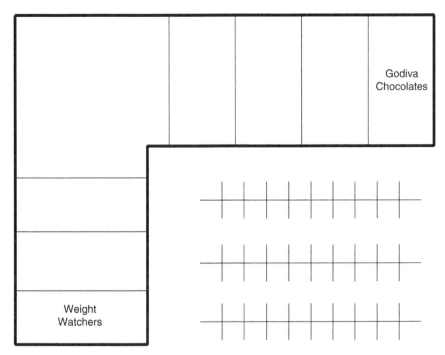

FIGURE 8.5 Good and Bad Tenant Placement: Example 2

questions as you now look at Figure 8.5. Is the tenant placement in Figure 8.5 better? The answer is that it's debatable, depending on what you are trying to achieve. Do you think the two stores are mutually exclusive and thus there is no competition? Or do you think the stores could feed off each other? That is, as people eat too much chocolate, they have to lose weight. Or if people become tired of dieting, they can splurge from time to time by purchasing some chocolate. It is a placement decision you need to make. In many ways, there is no correct or incorrect rationale. But you have to make a decision, and that decision will affect the overall value of the property.

Now, let us consider Figure 8.6, a site diagram of a very typical retail center with a movie theater as an anchor, a restaurant next door, and various other tenants. Is this a good layout? Many will say that this is a good layout because of the restaurant next to the movie theater—the so-called dinner and a movie. Unfortunately, this is a terrible layout and tenant placement because movie theaters are notorious for patrons who monopolize the parking spaces closest to the movie theater entrance. When this occurs, patrons of the restaurant have to park relatively far away. If the weather is unpleasant (rain or snow), patrons are discouraged from using this

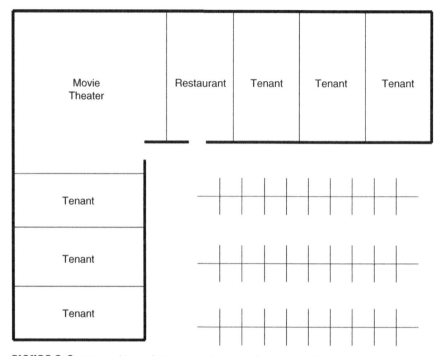

FIGURE 8.6   Typical Retail Center with an Anchor: Example 1

restaurant. If we consider the same site but slightly reconfigure the buildings such as in Figure 8.7, the movie theater's entrance is in the back of the retail center with corresponding parking spaces. In this configuration, patrons of the movie theater are directed away from the parking spaces in front of the retail center and allow adequate parking for the restaurant and other tenants in the retail center. For those patrons who do like the idea of a dinner and a movie, the restaurant also has a rear entrance so that patrons can park in the rear of the retail center, have a meal, and then see a movie. In the first instance, Figure 8.6, such a layout would negatively affect the overall value of the retail center because patrons who are inconvenienced are unlikely to visit the retail center as often as they otherwise might. Correspondingly, in Figure 8.7, the value of the retail center is enhanced because the design and layout of the buildings on the site provide a more pleasant experience for the patrons of the retail center.

The idea of tenant placement also applies to a regional mall or a town center. Figure 8.8 is a town center configuration with an anchor flanked by two rows of in-line stores. The closer in-line stores would pay a higher rent

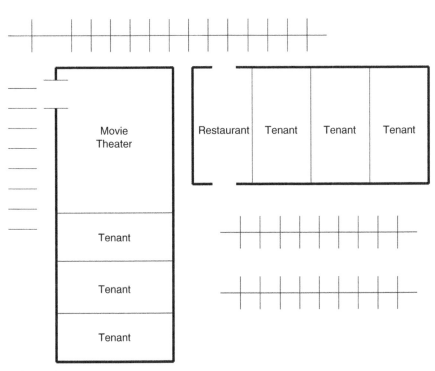

FIGURE 8.7 Better Retail Center Layout

per square foot because of their physical closeness to the large anchor with the advantage of the foot traffic. A retail store furthest away from the anchor would have a relatively lower rent per square foot because of the distance from the entrance to the anchor store and arguably be exposed to a lesser traffic flow. Another aspect of tenant placement in the situation in Figure 8.8 is that in-line tenants will be allowed to be located close to the anchor tenant's entrance. Often as part of the lease negotiations for an anchor tenant, the anchor tenant specifies which retail stores cannot be located near that anchor's front entrance (direct competitors). We discuss this point more later in the book on the topic of leases.

I have been discussing tenant placement concepts in a retail environment. Tenant placement concepts are just as applicable in an office building environment. There, tenant placement concepts are subtler and often include considerations of space overlap when expansion space or option space is a factor. In this situation, it is very important and valuable to have a good and experienced leasing broker to help you avoid inadvertent bad tenant placement decisions.

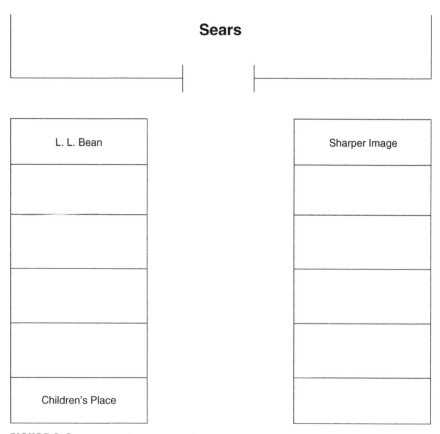

FIGURE 8.8   Tenant Placement with a Town Center

"The reward for work well done is the opportunity to do more."
—Jonas Salk

I would like to reiterate a concept and one of my clichés. When selecting tenants for your building, you certainly have to be cognizant of tenant placement, as we have been discussing. However, each tenant is a business unto its own. As such, each tenant is in a particular market or market segment, and the lease that you negotiate contributes to the income and cash flow of the building, leading to value. So, if you understand how stocks operate in a stock investment portfolio, you should then understand that a building is nothing more than a lease portfolio. The lease portfolio or building has characteristics of risk, yield, diversification, and concentration. If you choose tenants with a high-risk profile—say, filling your retail center with all mom-and-pop stores—you will have higher rent revenue, but the risk of a high vacancy rate in your retail center is higher than if you had a mix of mom-and-pop stores and the national stores. Similarly, in an office building, if you lease space to tenants all in the same industry, and that industry has an economic downturn, you more than likely will suffer higher vacancies and thus lower cash flow and value for the building. "A building is nothing more than a portfolio of leases" So it should be clear at this point that the tenants you choose and where you place the tenants are very important decisions directly affecting the overall value of your building and your portfolio of leases.

A BRIEF WORD ABOUT ARCHITECTURAL DRAWINGS

This section may seem out of place in this chapter; however, I want readers to understand the flow of architectural drawings when we discuss them later in the book. There are three basic types of architectural drawings in a development project:

1. Schematic design.
2. Design development.
3. Construction documents.

Schematic design drawings are very rough drawings illustrating ideas of mass and shape for the developer. Schematic design drawings can range from near line scratches on the back of a napkin to fairly detailed drawings. With them, a developer tries to envision the project and incorporate every possible feature to accommodate the site and prospective tenants. The schematic design drawings are detailed enough, though, to prepare preliminary development cost budgets.

Once the iterations of schematic design drawings are complete and the developer is relatively satisfied with the design of the proposed project, the architect will move toward creating the design development drawing. Design development drawings take the schematic design drawings and bring them to scale and introduce colors, materials, and floor space layouts. In the case of mixed-use project, some of the components may be introduced and then eliminated to test the sensitivity of the development cost and projected values. Design development drawings may also change a number of times but hopefully not as often as the schematic design drawings. Needless to say, the developer can further refine the development cost budget at this point. Once the developer is satisfied with the design development drawings, then the developer gives approval to the architect to begin construction documents.

Construction documents are the architectural drawings in complete detail; they allow a contractor to physically build the building. Sometimes people refer to these construction documents as blueprints. When the construction documents are approximately 60 percent, 70 percent, or 80 percent completed, they are referred to as bid drawings. The developer includes these drawings in requests for proposals or in solicitations for cost bids from contractors for the project.

LEARNING POINTS FROM THIS CHAPTER

After reading this chapter, I should:

- Understand how and why the elements of design are used for both site selection and project programming and design.
- Learn one of the more common and better methods of gathering information necessary for the programming and design of your project.
- Understand the importance of tenant mix and marketability.
- Know the basic architectural drawing flow.

CHAPTER 9

Entitlement Process and Public-Private Partnerships

We spoke about zoning and typical zoning categories in an earlier chapter. A key part of the community approval process, otherwise known as the entitlement process, is to understand the government's and community's political climate. You should ask questions of the community such as, What is going on? Who has influence in the community and government? How does something occur? What is the typical timing?

In the same vein, you should learn about the public approval process by asking similar how, what, and when questions. Asking these questions will give you answers about the entitlement process. The entitlement process is similar everywhere, but the detailed process is very different in each location. Thus, it is essential to ask these questions in every community where you plan to do a real estate development.

The government, while its actions often appear at odds with developers, actually needs and looks to the real estate industry to revitalize and generate jobs and taxes. The two groups are often at odds due to the lack of understanding of each other's needs, constraints, and resources. The area in which the government and developers come to understand each other and agree to work together toward a common goal is called a public-private partnership.

TYPICAL COMMUNITY APPROVAL PROCESS

Every community—whether it is New York, Beijing, or Des Moines, Iowa—has a slightly different entitlement or public approval process. That said, the entitlement process does follow a fairly standard flow, as shown in Figure 9.1. If you understand the typical entitlement process as described in Figure 9.1, you will have a good idea of how to proceed in any community around the world.

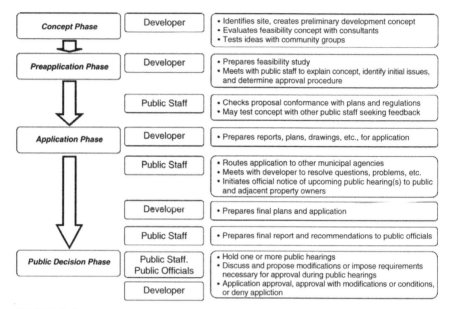

FIGURE 9.1 Typical Entitlement Process

The typical entitlement process has four phases:

1. A concept phase.
2. The preapplication phase.
3. The application phase.
4. The public approval phase.

The concept phase is all about the developer. Just as we described in the overall development process, the developer in the concept phase of the entitlement process identifies the site, prepares preliminary drawings, and evaluates the feasibility of the project, all the while testing his ideas with community groups and the government. Testing your ideas with community groups and the government is very, very important—no, it is essential! Many developers overlook or consciously skip this step, but developers often learn very quickly that their proposed plans will be stymied by community groups or the government for no other reason than that they were excluded from the overall planning process.

In the preapplication phase of the entitlement process, you are in the feasibility phase of the development process. You are drafting your project's business plan or feasibility report. While doing so, you should be having an active dialogue with the government and community about the various aspects of your proposed project, listening to feedback and criticism, and negotiating and compromising various points. As decisions are reached, you then incorporate those points into your proposed project program and design. During this preapplication phase of the entitlement process, you have active dialogues with various agencies of the government and check your proposed plans against existing regulations and ordinances.

As the parties during the preapplication phase become satisfied with various aspects of your proposed project, you then move into the application phase of the entitlement process. In the application phase, a formal application for approval of your proposed project is made to the government. If you did your job correctly, there should be very little criticism from the government at this point because you as a developer had a proactive discussion with the government (and community) during the preapplication phase. The application phase is very important as well because it leads to the government initially approving your project and then scheduling a public hearing.

In the public hearing phase, once again, if you took a proactive role during the preapplication phase by having a dialogue with the community as well as the government, the community should already be supportive of your project. Of course, there may be various questions regarding aspects of your project during the public hearings, but given your previous conversations with the community, there should be no real opposition to your proposed project (you cannot please everyone, especially NIMBYs). During a public hearing phase, the government in response to the feedback from the community will offer one of three decisions: approval of your project as proposed, approval of your project given certain conditions (which would result in a subsequent public hearing), or denial of approval for your proposed project.

PUBLIC-PRIVATE PARTNERSHIPS

The government and community take an active interest in what you do as a developer. There is a clear rationale for the public's interest in creating a public-private partnership with you. The government in particular is very aware that a reduction of jobs in the community is detrimental to that community. As jobs are lost in the community, the community experiences problems such as fiscal distress (lowered property tax revenues) and social dysfunction (crime). The government recognizes that real estate is a major asset on the balance sheet of the community. So the government has decided that it is appropriate to focus on real estate investment when trying to raise property tax revenues and reduce crime. As such, the government often offers tax incentives to businesses (who then contact developers) to relocate within their community.

> *"In my case, if one out of five opportunities is interesting enough to work on, maybe one in five of those ends up being worth doing. That might be a function of risk. That might be a function of price. There are all the variables. But you have to be constantly sorting and choosing and prioritizing."*
>
> —Sam Zell

Forming a public-private partnership with the government is fairly straightforward and has significant benefits. First, a public-private partnership involves the private sector much earlier in the process. If you remember what was described during the preapplication phase of the entitlement process, most important is an active conversation between you and the government. As this active conversation occurs, feedback and criticisms of all involved are incorporated into the proposed project, resulting in all parties buying into the proposed project. Another advantage of the public-private partnership is that relatively limited public resources are used. For example, you will more likely than not be required to submit a traffic impact study with your application to the government. If the government, while reviewing your traffic impact study, disagrees with an aspect of that study, the government will hire its own consultant to either confirm or refute your study. In essence, this is a duplication of expense. While working with the government in establishing a public-private partnership, you and the government could agree on a common traffic impact study and save roughly half of the total cost spent by both parties.

I cannot overemphasize the importance of having a proactive discussion with the government and the resulting public commitments to support your project. In one project I worked on several years ago, the mayor of the town was so enthusiastic about our proposed project that he personally contacted individuals within the community to ask for their support of my project. This marketing of my proposed project was extremely powerful and did not increase my costs—on the contrary, it saved money. However, while you are establishing a public-private partnership and having proactive discussions with the government, you and the government should be quite aware of any concern regarding independence or a perceived collusion. The worst thing that could happen as part of a public-private partnership is for your government contacts to read the morning newspaper and see headlines stating that you the developer and the government are working together unfairly to the community. The simplest and most effective solution for this potential problem is transparency. I recommend that any time you have a conversation with the government regarding a significant aspect of your proposed project, that you issue a press release summarizing the conversation. In doing so, at least you gave the clear impression that no information is being hidden from the community.

When working with the government and the community, you first need to understand the terminology. For example, a government contact may talk about impact fees, exaction fees, or linkage fees. The three terms essentially mean the same thing. These are fees charged to a developer because a developer's proposed project will have a so-called impact on the community just by its existence, such as the need for improved roads or utility systems for a larger or improved building, or, in the case of a multifamily residential project, the increased number of children in the community who will need school facilities.

As you approach a community and its government, you will see that they have a view of three different types of development projects. The first type of development project is a project that is privately fundable and does not need any government assistance. In this case, you pursue your proposed project through the entitlement process but ask for no tax abatements, no financial assistance, and minimal if any zoning variance requests. The second type of development project is a nonviable development project. We all saw lots of nonviable projects prior to the 1980s, when many development projects were done solely for the purpose of generating income tax benefits. At the time, many of the projects that were built had no economic viability. Many had high vacancies and became a burden on the government and community as a result. The government has no interest in a nonviable development project. The third type of development project is a project that makes sense—a project that will improve a community by starting redevelopment of an area that has been in decline or takes an abandoned building and converts it into a feasible use. However, developers often find, in pursuing a worthy project, that they have difficulty getting support, particularly financial support. In this situation, the government can be very helpful to you because in this third type of development project, market failure exists. Market failure is justification for a public-sector role in worthy projects. As a result, the public sector is very interested in helping you develop your worthy project by providing subsidies to incentive you to proceed with your development plans.

What is a market failure and what causes market failure? There are four causes of real estate market failure: incomplete capital markets, monopolies, lack of information, and macroeconomic factors. Incomplete capital market is a fairly common situation. An example is when a developer pursuing a worthy project cannot finance its cost, resulting in a gap in the capital stack (financing). Proposing a worthy project in an economically distressed area is viewed very positively by government and the community. If you cannot raise the financing you need to fill the capital stack of the proposed project, even after reducing budget costs, the government can often provide tax abatements, grants, or low-interest loans to fill the gap. Many communities are dominated by a few local development companies or developers. These local companies create a monopolistic environment that often precludes new developers from doing projects in the community. Sure, monopolies are illegal, but these monopolistic developers can subtly and not so subtly place roadblocks that prevent a new developer from pursuing a project in the community. It is essential for you to have an open dialogue with the government and show the worth of your project. A government that is convinced of the worth of your project can take certain actions to ensure that your project gets approved.

> *"The silly question is the first intimation of some totally new development."*
> —Alfred North Whitehead, English mathematician and philosopher

Lack of information is another example of market failure, particularly when the worthy project is proposed for a pioneering area. Often a pioneering area has been in fiscal distress for some time. As a result, little if any market information has been accumulated by local brokers and economists. What many do not realize is that government is always surveying the population within its community, including the areas that are economically distressed. The information is often not publicly distributed, but it is public information. If while gathering the data for your proposed project, you find that you lack certain market data, again, you should have a conversation with your government contact, who can often make the data available to you. The last cause of market failure is macroeconomic factors, such as rising interest rates or installation. The macroeconomic factors usually cause higher development costs (because of a higher interest rate) or lower than expected market value, often resulting in a gap in your project's capital stack. A government convinced of the worth of your project could then offer you tax abatements, grants, or low-interest loans to fill the gap in your project's capital stack.

So, really, what is going to motivate a government to offer you incentives for your proposed project? Benefits. Identify the benefits to the government and the community. Be specific in identifying the benefits and quantify each one of them as best you can. For example, one of the most common benefits that we've been talking about is the benefit of increased property tax revenues from new or renovated real estate projects. Another common benefit for the government and the community is the creation of jobs: temporary jobs during construction and later permanent jobs. Another obvious benefit is the improvement in the community where people live, work, and play. Quantifying this last benefit is a little difficult, but estimating the incremental increase in property taxes and jobs created is fairly straightforward. But the one question that everyone has is What's in it for me? No one in the government or the community is going to give approval or consent for a proposed project unless they have a good understanding of what they are going to gain or benefit from it. Important to both the community and the government is the increase in incremental property taxes for two reasons:

1. The government will be able to finance various other projects throughout the community.
2. The community will have reduced residential real estate taxes because of increased commercial property real estate taxes in the community.

The justification for a public-private partnership for the government is that the government wants to achieve certain improvements in the community to make its assets productive from a revenue perspective. That being said, you should realize that worthy projects often have problems, such as environmental contamination requiring remediation. But for the government, incentivizing a developer to remediate a site is very important because often remediation of a site will start to execute the government's vision for the city and serve as a catalyst for additional development.

Other government incentives could include, but are not limited to:

- Property tax abatement
- Public sector equity
- Public sector debt (in the form of tax-exempt bonds or tax increment financing)
- Credit enhancement or insurance
- Housing, historic preservation, job credits, and other tax incentives

Pragmatically, while detailing and quantifying the benefits of a proposed project, you should also detail the associated costs. Several associated costs may arise from the incremental tax revenues, such as the widening of the road leading up to a new project due to increased automobile traffic flow. By listing both the benefits and the costs, you essentially answer many objections that may arise as a result of your proposed project. (Hopefully, the benefits will far outweigh the costs listed. If not, you need to reprogram and/or redesign your project.)

If a government wants to be proactive with a public-private partnership, it often initiates the process by soliciting developers through a request for proposal (RFP).

When speaking to the government and the community, constantly remind them—each time you speak to them—of the benefits that your proposed project will generate. People in any environment tend to have short memories. As a result, reminding the people you speak to about the benefits—what's in it for them—is very important. And again, when mentioning these benefits, be sure to quantify them. For example, it's one thing to say that incremental property taxes will be increased in the community, and it's another thing to say that incremental property taxes will be increased by US $1 million annually. Mentioning these benefits when speaking to anyone in the government or the community has a compelling impact that benefits you and your proposed project.

LEARNING POINTS FROM THIS CHAPTER

After reading this chapter, I should:

- Understand the steps of the government entitlement process.
- Know the four reasons for market failure.
- Learn some of the common benefits or subsidies provided by a government to a developer.
- Understand the importance of answering the question, What's in it for me?

CHAPTER 10

Budgeting, Financial Analysis, and Capital Structure

A primer of financial analysis and budgeting is not within the scope of this book, so this chapter, like others in this book, addresses the chapter topic from the perspective of the developer; that is, how does a developer use and interpret the information as it is being created or interpret the information after it has been created?

PREPARING FOR THE FINANCIAL ANALYSIS AND PRO FORMA

Capital and operating budgets are revised as necessary, and as often as necessary, to provide the returns desired by investors. We learned in school to start with the revenues, subtract expenses, and end up with the net operating income. We can calculate the net present value of the operating income by applying a capitalization rate to create a value. We also use the net operating income to calculate the return on equity for investors. We all learned this methodology in school; however, in reality we actually work backward. Say we have an investor who is willing to give us US$1 million and requires a 10 percent return. That means that if we wish to obtain the investor's money, we must find projects that generate an annual net operating income of US$100,000. From this net operating income, we know what the market expenses are, and then add those expenses to the net operating income to equal the total revenues. By calculating our operating pro forma backward, we establish benchmark targets, such as rental rate and concession targets. We benchmark results of our operating pro forma against similar projects we have done or against similar projects in the market. In essence, by working our operating pro forma backward, we are testing financing achievability.

THE DEVELOPMENT BUDGET

The following list shows the typical categories included in a development budget. A common mistake many beginning developers make is thinking that the development cost equals the construction cost. The construction cost is only a small part of the development cost or budget. A development budget includes the construction cost (hard cost), as well as land, architectural fees, engineering fees, marketing costs, and financing costs. A development budget also includes a development fee, which is how a developer earns money during the development process to cover business operating costs and personal living costs. It can range from as little as 0.5 percent to 10 percent or more. A development fee is calculated by taking the percentage mentioned in the previous sentence and applying it to the total eventual development cost budget. The development fee percentage typically is inversely related to the amount of the development cost budget; that is, the larger the development cost, the smaller the development fee percentage. Conversely, the lower the development cost, the larger the development fee percentage. There is no set amount of development fee charged by a developer. One little trick that a developer uses relative to the development fee is including the maximum development fee in the initial budget. If the investor returns are not being met, and other cost savings have been identified, the developer might reduce the development fee to a point where the investor returns are met—essentially, plugging the development fee into the budget. The line items in the following list are typical line items. You might, in your specific proposed project, add or subtract various line items as appropriate. The rule of thumb for line items is to include those line items you want to manage during the development process or include line items that are unique and significant in cost for your particular proposed project.

Development Budget Line Items

Land cost
Site development costs
Design fees
  ■ Architecture
  ■ Engineering

Hard costs
  ■ By category
  ■ Labor and materials
Permitting costs
Financing costs
  ■ Loan fees
  ■ Construction interest

Marketing costs
  ■ Promotion and advertising
  ■ Leasing commissions
  ■ Broker's fees
Preopening operating costs
Real estate taxes
Insurance
Legal fees
Accounting costs
Field supervision (inspection) costs
Development fees
Contingencies

In addition to preparing the total development cost budget, you will also need to prepare a draw schedule for the (probably monthly) timing of project cash flows and inflows and the timing of financing outflows and inflows, resulting in loan interest calculations and investor waterfall calculations.

THE OPERATING PRO FORMA

The next list shows the typical categories included in an operating pro forma. The line items in the development project in this list are typical line items. You might, in your specific proposed project, add or subtract line items as appropriate. The rule of thumb is including line items for what you want to manage during the development process.

Operating Pro Forma Budget

Base rental revenues	Vacancy/credit loss
	Common area maintenance
Percentage rent	Real estate taxes
CAM revenue	Insurance
Garage revenue	Management fee
Miscellaneous revenue	Operating reserve
■ Laundry	Capital reserve
■ Telephone	Loan interest
■ Antenna	
■ Billboards	

In addition to preparing the total operating pro forma, you will need to prepare a monthly operating pro forma for the timing of (probably monthly)project cash flows and inflows and the timing of financing outflows and inflows, resulting in loan interest calculations and investor waterfall calculations.

REVIEW OF COMMON ANALYTICAL MEASUREMENTS

Key ratios are regularly used to analyze development projects. The ratios standardize the numbers and facilitate comparisons among different iterations of the pro formas of different but similar projects. The ratios highlight weaknesses and strengths in your project. The major categories of ratios used include:

- Liquidity ratios.
- Profitability ratios.
- Asset (returns) ratios.
- Debt (financing) ratios.
- Valuation ratios.

In this chapter, I focus on asset and debt ratios. All of the ratios are important, but you will use the asset and debt ratios on almost a daily basis. The asset ratios include:

- Hurdle rate.
- Cash-on-cash return.
- Return on assets.
- Return on equity.
- Payback period.

The hurdle rate is the minimum acceptable return for the investor. Typically, the hurdle rate is the weighted average cost of capital. If you consider that the hurdle rate is equal to the weighted average cost of capital, what you have is really break even. I do not know many people who are in business, other than not-for-profits, simply to break even. As discussed in an earlier chapter, there are four things that comprise a useful hurdle rate: (1) the weighted average cost of capital, plus (2) the opportunity cost of investing in this particular project, plus (3) a risk factor given the type of project being considered, and (4) desired profit. Some argue that the opportunity cost, risk factor, and desired profit are already included in the weighted average cost of capital calculation. While this is true, the opportunity cost, risk cost, and profit are those of the investor giving you the money, not your opportunity cost, risk cost, and profit. Now, when you've calculated a useful hurdle rate and the calculated return from a proposed project exceeds your useful hurdle rate, you know for a fact that this is a good investment for you. The useful hurdle rate is a personal calculation for each individual investor. I encourage you to calculate your own useful hurdle rate and use it on a regular basis. You might even calculate a useful hurdle rate for different property types and geographic locations. Having multiple useful hurdle rates for different circumstances is not unusual.

> *"Predicting rents and occupancy levels is easy. We've been doing it for 20 years. Predicting interest rates is a whole other ballgame."*
> —Ray Torto, principal and chief strategist, Torto Wheaton Research, CBRE World Conference, September 9, 2004

The cash-on-cash return is a simple calculation taking one year's net operating income and dividing it by the equity invested. Since this is a one-year calculation, there is no present value consideration in the calculation. The cash-on-cash return is often used by brokers to entice buyers to a property. Unfortunately, the calculation is often misleading because it would not give, say, an indication that all of the leases in the building are expiring the following year.

The return on assets calculation is not useful to a developer per se, but it is used by lenders, which makes it an important ratio for developers. Return on assets is calculated by dividing the net operating income by the total property cost. Since you are using the total property cost, no leverage (use of debt) is being considered, and often it can be a more realistic indication of the property's financial performance.

Return on equity is frequently used and is calculated by dividing the net present value of the property's net operating income by the initial equity invested in the property. Let's say that we are analyzing an operating property with an amortizing mortgage. Does it make sense that the return-on-equity calculation is the net present value of the property's net operating income divided by the initial equity *plus* the first years of mortgage amortization? It does, because by the time you know what the annual net operating income is, a year's worth of principal payments would have been made, adding to the equity invested in the project. The point of mentioning this second example of the calculation of return on equity is that you should always ask how a ratio has been calculated.

Many people in firms tend to customize their measurement ratios. The second calculation for return on equity in the previous paragraph is one example of how the traditional calculation could be modified. Neither calculation is wrong. To make a good decision, you must inquire how the ratios were calculated so that you will be comparing apples to apples.

You might also use a payback period calculation, which calculates the amount of time it takes to recover your equity investment. To calculate the payback period, you divide the equity investment by the net operating income over a period of time (could be done on a net present value basis). The payback period was often used for pioneering projects where a developer was uncertain of ever recovering the equity investment in the project. Today, while the calculation is still used in a similar manner, it is often used in highly structured transactions where the developer's equity is highly subordinated in the capital structure, and there is a fairly small chance of ever recovering the equity investment.

The financing ratios include:

* Mortgage (loan) constant.
* Loan amortization.
* Capitalization rate.
* Loan-to-value ratio.
* Debt service ratio.

The mortgage constant is calculated by dividing the annual debt service (interest and/or principal) by the original loan amount. The mortgage constant is an important ratio used to compare different loan structures and bring them to an apples-to-apples basis. The higher the resulting percentage from calculating the mortgage constant, the greater the financial load on the net operating income of the project. Thus, the resultant mortgage loan constant calculated for different loan structures will help you decide which loan structure to accept for your project.

Loan amortization is the repayment of the loan principal over the term of the loan. Loan amortization is viewed favorably by a lender, whose risk of repayment is reduced over time. Not all loans are amortized; some are interest-only.

> *"Apply yourself. Get all the education you can, but then, by God, do something. Don't just stand there—make it happen."*
>
> —Lee Iacocca

The capitalization rate is used to value commercial properties. It is calculated by dividing the net present value of the net operating income of the project by the appropriate capitalization rate to get the estimated value of the project. While there is a fairly detailed calculation method for deriving the capitalization rate, more often than not, it is determined by looking at recent property sales and dividing the property sales price by the net present value of the net operating income at the time the sale occurred.

The loan-to-value ratio is calculated by dividing the loan amount by the property's value. Lenders often have a maximum loan-to-value ratio for different property types. If you are working on a development project—that is, a project that has yet to be built—you would use a loan-to-cost ratio. A loan-to-cost ratio is calculated like the loan-to-value ratio except that you divide the projected pro forma net present value of the net operating income by the total development costs.

The debt service ratio is calculated by taking the net operating income for a given period, typically a year, and dividing it by the total debt service (interest and/or principal). Banks often have a minimum debt service ratio for different property types. Typically, the debt service ratio required by a bank changes more than the bank's loan-to-value ratio for different property types.

FINANCING AND THE CAPITAL MARKETS

As you calculate the development budget and operating pro forma for a proposed project, you are essentially starting the financing and lending sequence. The financing and lending sequence is not unlike the development process in that there are distinct phases:

- Bright idea.
- Idea development.
- Land acquisition.
- Funding construction (construction alone).
- Permanent financing.
- Subsequent financing.

The first phase of the financing and lending sequence is getting a bright idea. In getting your bright idea, you are thinking about different sites and different ideas for those sites. So, you find a property and explore the various possibilities. While very little money is spent at this time, any cost is totally funded by you the developer.

The next phase of the financing and lending sequence is developing your idea. It is during this phase that you are likely to spend money on various consultants for design, environmental, and architectural ideas. Be very careful about how much money you spend on your proposed project because there is no certainty that your project will continue, and there is no certainty that you will be able to recover the costs invested. If you remember from the discussion of the enterprise concept, it is during this stage when developers experience the problem of short-term solvency. Some inexperienced or less disciplined developers spend a lot of money investigating a proposed site and developing their ideas with seemingly no perception that their project will not be moving forward or getting approval, thus losing any monies invested. As a result, many beginning or undisciplined developers enter bankruptcy at this stage. So the general rule of thumb is that you should not spend any money unless you know that by spending that money you will create value and have something to sell. Nevertheless, any money needed at this stage is totally funded by the developer. Certainly the developer can raise money from friends and family, use credit cards, or obtain a home equity loan, but you will not be able to raise money from third parties at this time.

Land or property acquisition typically occurs in the third phase of the financing and lending sequence. There is good and bad news at this stage. The good news is that you will be able to obtain a project-based or land acquisition loan for the first time. The bad news is that it is very difficult to obtain a land acquisition loan. Typically the loan-to-value for a land acquisition loan is very low, between 30 and 50 percent. Land acquisition loans are very difficult to obtain. Unless you are an experienced homebuilder with experience converting land acquisitions into home sales in a very short time, it is unlikely that you will get a land loan for your project. Even if you do obtain a land loan for your project with a loan-to-value ratio of 30 to 50 percent, you still have to come up with equity ranging from 70 to 50 percent. This equity money will be funded by you, the developer.

You might be able to secure an option for the purchase of the land, but you still would have to pay for the amount of the option payment. You may not have short-term solvency concerns during the idea development phase, but there is a strong possibility you are likely to have short-term solvency issues during the land acquisition phase.

The fourth phase of the financing and lending sequence is the funding of a construction loan. This is when every developer stays awake waiting because this is when the developer who invested monies for consultants and perhaps an option payment on the land can now get those costs reimbursed from the first draw of the construction loan as legitimate project costs. In other words, for the first time you will be able to pull some of your equity out of the project. But this is not quite as easy as it sounds. The construction loan typically has some conditions precedent for the first loan funding. A common condition precedent is the prelease or presale of space in the building. The bank will have its requirement of what the preleasing or presale levels should be; however, the level frequently depends on the type of property, the point at which we are in the real estate cycle, the bank's and investor's credit policy, and other factors. Many developers complain that the preleasing or presale level is too high. The reality is that a project that has preleasing or presales is a better project that will be able to sustain a market downturn as the project is in construction or in the initial occupancy phase.

I suggest that, rather than religiously following the bank-required preleasing or presale level, you should calculate what you want as minimum preleasing or presales. You determine that by working your operating pro forma backward; that is, determine the amount of preleasing or presales that would give the project a minimum debt coverage ratio. If you follow this approach, your project will still cash flow and be able to cover its debt, despite a downturn in the market cycle, slower than expected preleasing, or poor sales.

A second common condition precedent is a takeout commitment. A takeout commitment, or a commitment for future financing, substantially reduces the risk of the construction loan lender. Typically, a takeout commitment is provided by a long-term lender such as an insurance company or pension fund. About 10 years ago, a takeout commitment was required by construction lenders before the construction lender would provide a construction loan to a borrower. However, there have been several situations where the takeout lender, typically for a portfolio reason, did not fund the takeout commitment. So in today's world, the following statement usually applies: Having a takeout commitment does not help, but it may hurt your financing effort if you do not have it.

The last phase of the financing and lending cycle is subsequent refinancing. It may be refinancing the construction loan with permanent financing, or refinancing existing permanent financing to either increase the amount or obtain more favorable terms and conditions. It is through this refinancing that a developer can typically get equity out of the deal and perhaps some extra cash. Because the refinancing of a project is typically based on the value as opposed to the development cost of the project, refinancing proceeds can be obtained to repay the construction loan and have some extra cash out of the transaction.

There are typically two general types of permanent financing: a permanent loan or a mini-perm loan. A permanent loan is what you would imagine it would be, a loan based on the operating cash flows of an existing project, and it is typically long-term. It could be interest-only; more likely, it has an amortization of principal. A hybrid type of permanent financing is a mini-perm loan. A mini-perm loan includes the features of both a construction loan and a permanent loan. So, for example, let's say we have a project with a 24-month construction loan, and we obtain a five-year mini-perm loan. For the first two years of the mini-perm loan, it would operate just like any construction loan with monthly loan draws. Once certain conditions are met, such as preleasing or a minimum debt service coverage ratio, the loan converts into a permanent loan for the remaining three years of the five-year period. Mini-perm loans are not always available because they are based on the market cycle and the lender's confidence that the cycle is upward. The lender wants to see an upward market cycle because of its underwriting for a longer period (five years) instead of a short-term construction loan. A mini-perm loan is extremely attractive to a developer because as construction finishes, the developer is focused on obtaining a permanent loan to repay a maturing construction loan. If the market cycle has weakened for whatever reason, however, the developer may not be able to get a permanent loan in the amount necessary to repay the construction loan, may not be able to get the permanent loan when needed, or may not be able to get permanent financing at all. A mini-perm loan releases a lot of a developer's financing pressure at a time when the developer needs to be focused on other things, such as leasing the building.

SHORT- AND LONG-TERM FINANCING

Helpful to understanding the different types of short- and long-term financing available to you is a knowledge of the drivers in our financial markets. The diagram in Figure 10.1 provides a visual representation of these drivers, which in the real estate market cycle are circular. If we start with new real estate construction, the construction business is active, and much development is occurring. Then the market starts to right itself, and players in the market tend to focus on projects' financial feasibility. Often what you'll hear is a comment like "Let's sharpen our pencils," indicating that financing or budgets have become more difficult to manage.

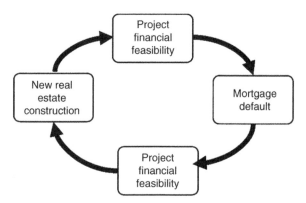

FIGURE 10.1 Drivers in Financial Markets

Eventually, the markets tighten to the extent that new development essentially stops, and we enter a period of mortgage defaults. When weak projects and their related mortgages are worked out of the markets, once again developers focus on their financing achievability and budgets. Then the markets revive, and active development occurs again. Needless to say, these drivers in the cycle are different for every market and for every property type within each market.

As we start to think about raising money for our project, we need to consider some sources of debt funds.

- Banks and savings and loans.
- Pension funds and endowments.
- Life insurance companies.
- Financial subsidiaries of manufacturing companies.
- REITs.
- Foreign investors.
- Funds (opportunity funds, hedge funds, and so forth).

Given these sources of debt funds, what are some sources of equity funds?

- Pension funds and endowments.
- Life insurance companies.
- Public or private limited partnerships.
- Developers and/or joint ventures.
- REITs.
- Foreign investors.
- Funds (opportunity funds, hedge funds, and so forth).

If you look at these two lists, with minor exceptions they are essentially the same. The biggest difference between the two lists is that commercial banks and savings and loans can provide only debt funds and cannot make equity investments (a U.S. requirement). While commercial banks and savings and loans may have affiliates that can provide equity funds, they are precluded by law in the United States for making equity investments.

So who would you go to for financing for your project?

- Commercial banks.
- Insurance companies.
- Pension funds.
- Private investors.
- Governments.

Each of the investors or players has distinct motivations when providing funds for development projects. The concept that supports the motivation of each of these investors is match funding. Match funding matches the tenor of their cash inflows with the tenor of the loans or investments they make. For example, commercial banks source their money from deposits; savings deposits are viewed as short-term money. Following the concept of match funding, commercial banks then lend money only short-term to mitigate interest rate risk. You would contact a commercial bank for a construction loan (short-term). On the other hand, insurance companies source their money from insurance premium payments; these payments are considered long-term. You would not contact an insurance company if you want a construction loan because an insurance company cannot properly match fund their money inflows with the outflows. Insurance companies are interested in long-term or permanent loans. Private investors source their money from just about anywhere. Therefore, private investors could make short- or long-term loans. Governments obtain their funding from tax revenues, and these taxes revenues are typically viewed as long-term.

In addition to match funding, these (debt) investors are further categorized into:

- Fiduciary lenders.
- Semifiduciary lenders.
- Nonfiduciary lenders.

The only fiduciary lender is a commercial bank. Commercial banks have a fiduciary responsibility to their investors or depositors. They have to return 100 percent of a depositor's money on demand. Thus commercial banks cannot make risky investments or loans. As a result, commercial banks typically make only straightforward, simple loans. If you are seeking a complex loan or a loan for a pioneering project, you would not go to a commercial bank.

Semifiduciary lenders include merchant banks and perhaps REITs. They have a responsibility to their equity investors. Equity investors are never promised a return on their investment, or a return of their capital investment, for that matter. Semifiduciary lenders will not make irresponsible loans, but they are more flexible in the types of loans they make and their loan structures.

Nonfiduciary lenders, which include individuals, private loan companies, and foreign funding sources, generally do not have any restrictions other than those they place on themselves. Thus, nonfiduciary lenders tend to be the most flexible and most willing to take risks of these three categories of lenders.

From this point, you should understand that there is a vast variety of loan structures and features that can be offered to you for your development project. It is wise to be proactive with lenders and lending brokers. Too many developers focus on preparing a financial pro forma and then sending copies to various lenders and brokers and asking them to provide their so-called best deal. When developers do this, the best deal they receive is not the best deal for them, but the best deal for the lender or the broker. You should decide, based upon your financial pro forma, on the best financial structure in the sense of terms and conditions for your development project. For example, you can match initially lower net cash flow numbers with, say, an interest-only loan for the first two or three years and then transition the mortgage terms to include principal and interest when a property's cash flows are stronger and can provide adequate debt service coverage.

To be proactive in your financing, you must be very familiar with the available loan structures and features available, which requires actively networking with a variety of investors. Detailed examples of loan structures are beyond the scope of this book, but I encourage you to learn as much as you possibly can about the financing available to you for your project.

Various tax credits and grants may be available from the federal and state governments. Often these programs come to light when working on a public-private partnership. These programs range from historical tax credits to low-income housing. Some of the programs that are available are direct programs, that is, programs that are offered directly to the borrower or user; there are also indirect programs, which are provided to the lending sources that then pass on the benefits to the borrower or user. All of these programs have eligibility requirements to meet. I have seen several development projects where almost 20 percent to 30 percent of the total capital for the project was provided by federal and state tax credit and grant programs. These programs should not be ignored.

One of the most useful programs is tax increment financing (TIF). As you prepare a financial pro forma for a proposed project, you will be able to determine what the incremental tax revenues might be for your new project. These incremental tax revenues would, at a minimum, be property taxes and perhaps sales taxes. The relevant municipality then calculates the incremental amount and issues bonds in the amount of the tax increment. The proceeds from the bond sale are given to the developer to use for the proposed project. The developer pays interest on the bond at the municipal interest rate and repays principal on the bonds once the project is operating and paying property taxes and perhaps also sales taxes. This is a very simplistic definition of TIF bonds, but consider the fact that every municipality in America has the capability of issuing TIF bonds.

FINANCING CYCLE—ANTICIPATING REQUIREMENTS

After several years of experience, you will start to recognize certain markers in the industry that can be used as indictors of what is likely to happen. As a result, you may be able anticipate financing requirements and thus the timing of your development project. Figure 10.2 illustrates a financing cycle.

As you look at the cycle, you can draw a line horizontally through the cycle indicating the average or so-called normal market. Starting at the left side, as the cycle moves upward (a better market), note that financing requirements tend to decrease. That's because as the market strengthens, lenders compete for business and/or eliminate or loosen their underwriting and loan requirements to obtain business. As the market cycle strengthens, mezzanine financing appears. Actually, mezzanine financing is always available, but there seems to be more available as the market strengthens. Developers often have distinct opinions at this point, such as there are so many projects that must be pursued and since capital is finite, the developer's capital has to be allocated among more projects and thus less capital for any given project is available. On the other hand, some experienced developers start to recognize that the market is strengthening and perhaps reaching its peak. As such, the developer wants to allocate available capital in case the peak is reached during the project development in order to not suffer any losses. Once

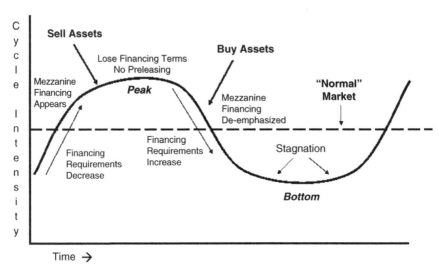

FIGURE 10.2 Financing Cycle—Anticipating Requirements

the cycle reaches a peak, there are virtually no loan covenants required, and you see the appearance of spec (speculative) buildings. Then the market cycle continues, and these characteristics reverse themselves. At some point at the bottom of the market cycle, there is stagnation, and only a few projects are being financed at all. These characteristics that appear in a market cycle are fairly reliable; however, there are times when the characteristics are not distinct and overlap. Nevertheless, if you are an asset holder, the best time to sell your assets is just before the market reaches its peak, when buyers still believe that there is an upside to the market and can justify purchasing assets. On the other hand, the best time to buy assets is after the peak and a bit further down in the cycle, as shown in the figure. Typically you would not be able to buy assets immediately after the peak of the cycle because many asset holders believe that any downturn in the market is temporary or just a blip. However, asset owners, after seeing that the downturn in the market is not a blip, become somewhat frantic and start to sell their assets at immediate discounts. This time along the cycle, between the peak and the time you should buy assets, is the time I call the period of denial.

I offer this financing cycle as a methodology for identifying where you are in the cycle and the characteristics that appear at that point and anticipating future requirements or trends. If you see these characteristics as outlined on Figure 10.2, you may be able to pinpoint where you are in the cycle and thus better plan the timing of your proposed project.

ELEMENTS OF A FEASIBILITY STUDY OR DEAL BOOK

A feasibility study is an essential task for any developer. It is a business plan for a specific proposed project, the summary of all the research and planning done by the developer. The feasibility study emphasizes information relevant to all the target audiences or constituencies.

Feasibility Study Table of Contents

- Executive summary.
- Project description.
- Benefits analysis.
- Renderings of proposed project.
- Location and area maps.
- Photographs of existing site and neighborhood.

- Site control and constraints.
- Market analysis.
- Marketability analysis.
- Detailed risk analysis with mitigation.
- Exit plans.
- Leasing plan.
- Marketing plan.
- Cash flow analyses.
  - Detailed development budget.
  - Detailed operating pro forma.
  - Capital structure.
- Development team and team biographies.
- Supporting and supplemental information, assumptions, reference, sources, bibliography.

As you can see, the study is quite comprehensive. Information ranges from the general to the specific, from construction through financial analysis. A key aspect of a feasibility study is the exit plan. An exit plan should be established for each of the six phases of the development process. When creating an exit plan, a useful approach is to ask yourself the question, What would happen if?

Despite the number of items that should be included in a feasibility study, only three sections are of ultimate importance: the marketability study, the benefit analysis, and the risk and mitigation analysis. They are what convince a constituency to approve or invest in a project. All of the other sections are background information (although they have to be completed in order to prepare the marketability study, the benefit analysis, and the risk and mitigation analysis).

Summarizing the marketability study detailed in an earlier chapter, it describes whether you *could* build the project and whether you *should* build the project. Once you've gone through the marketability study and can justify that you could and should build the project, you move on to the benefits analysis, which outlines the benefits to each of your five constituencies: the government, the community, the end users, the investors, and yourself.

As you outline the benefits to each of the five constituencies, specify and quantify each of the benefits to be derived. For example, if you determine that one of the benefits of your proposed project for the government is increased real estate taxes, you should estimate how much. You should also review the benefits each time you interact with the constituencies to reinforce the end result of benefits for them. You want to be proactive and answer the question that everyone has regarding whether to approve or invest in your project: What's in it for me?

You have now shown that your proposed project could be built and should be built, as well as the specific benefits to be derived from your proposed project for those who approve or invest in your project. Next, focus on the risk analysis. I have identified eight categories of risks for a real estate project (or any business, for that matter).

Categories of Risk

1. Business risk.
2. Management risk.
3. Financial risk.
4. Interest rate risk.
5. Liquidity risk.
6. Legislative risk.
7. Inflation risk.
8. Environmental risk.

As an aside, it is very important to identify risks for your project. Frankly, the process of identifying risks is very easy. What is more difficult is to define the mitigation for the risks. I have seen a number of risk analyses in which the risks have been competently identified, but there is no mention of any mitigation of the risks. The risk mitigation is extremely important, particularly if you are a beginning developer. By mitigating the risks—and *writing out* the mitigation in your feasibility study—you have two specific advantages. First, every question that any of your constituencies will ask you about your project will fall into one of the categories of risks. If, when asked a question, you can promptly respond with the mitigation for the risk (because you already have thought about and written out the mitigation), you give the impression that you have competently organized your project. Second, the process of writing out the risks and mitigation provides you with a self-checking mechanism. For example, you reach the interest rate risk category and identify that interest rates might increase over the term of your project development period. However, as you think of this risk, you realize that you have not done anything to mitigate the risk, such as incorporating an interest rate derivative product. So as a self-checking mechanism, this analysis forces you to identify a mitigation for each risk. Let's define each of these risks.

Business risk address the concern that your project will be unsuccessful given the choice of property type, project programming and design, location, and market. The typical mitigation of this business risk is comple-tion of a marketability study that shows demand for your proposed project as you have defined it.

Management risk is the risk of whether you and your project team are able to execute your business plan or feasibility study. As a new developer, you encounter a lot of skepticism about your ability to do so. The mitiga-tion for this risk is to surround yourself with experienced people, such as an experienced contractor and an experienced architect, to compensate for your personal lack of experience.

Financial risk is limited if your development budget and operating pro forma assumptions have been reasonably accurate (not including interest and inflation risks, which are addressed separately). One reality problem with your budgets and pro forma is that they are based on estimates, which may be wrong. So the financial risk addresses what measures you have taken to mitigate the possibility of your budgets and pro forma being wrong. For example, you might establish firm contracts of various types to lock in costs. Another standard mitigation is to do a sensitivity and scenario analysis, commonly known as a base and worst case analysis. To do this, you set parameters of expected outcomes. In this circumstance, we know that your budgeting and pro forma will be wrong, but at least you have a range of outcomes.

Interest rate risk, as we alluded to previously, is the risk that interest rates will rise during the development period. Needless to say, should inter-est rates rise, interest costs may exceed the budgeted amount. Should inter-est rates rise during the leasing or sale time, rising interest rates not only would become a burden on operations but may also curtail or at least slow down the leasing or sale effort. The mitigation for interest rate risk is to obtain fixed-interest-rate loans (which would only and possibly occur for a permanent mortgage) or use various interest rate financial derivative prod-ucts, such as interest rate swaps or interest rate caps.

Liquidity risk is the risk that you won't have the cash when you need the cash. There are four times in a development project when you have to be concerned about whether you have the necessary cash. The first is up to the point when you obtain a construction loan, otherwise known as short-term solvency. The second time you should be concerned about liquidity risk is getting the construction loan when you need it. The challenge in every development project is being able to close on the first draw of a con-struction loan when you need to pay your various consultants. The third time of liquidity risk is obtaining permanent financing to repay your con-struction loan when your construction loan matures. If the capital markets, for example, should be tight, you may have difficulty in obtaining a perma-nent loan in the amount and under the terms and conditions acceptable to you. Last, liquidity risk arises during operations when you might have a shortfall, and you have to be able to access a line of credit to cover that operating shortfall. A mitigation in all of these cases is preplanning your cash needs well in advance of the actual need by getting forward commitments or otherwise arranging the loan facilities well in advance of the need.

Legislative risk addresses changes in laws or regulations that could affect your project. Legislative risk arises twice during development: first, up until the point you receive all your entitlement approvals, and second, during operations of the project. Law and regulation changes during operations can affect your project, say, if they involve health and safety matters such as adapting access to meet ADA (Americans with Disabilities Act) standards. The mitigation for this risk is to maintain an active monitoring process at the municipality so that you can be made aware of upcoming changes as soon as possible.

Inflation risk is the risk of changes in the rate of inflation that affect the budgeted and operating costs of the project. Not unlike the mitigation for financial risk, you try to establish a variety of contracts to fix various budgeted and operating costs, and develop a sensitivity and scenario analysis to determine a range of financial outcomes.

> *"In 1988, when I was working as national security adviser for President Reagan, there was a lot of talk and concern about the Japanese buying up too much U.S. real estate. In a meeting, Reagan once said, 'Well, I'm glad they know good investments when they see them.'"*
> —Colin Powell, former secretary of state, speaking at AFIRE annual membership meeting, Washington, D.C., September 26, 2005

Environmental risk is the risk of current and future site contamination, as well as the risk associated with changes in the environment; that is, your project as built or renovated will change the surrounding community. The mitigation of environmental contamination is readily done by performing a phase 1 or a phase 2 environmental study. The effect on the community is often addressed by having an environmental impact study performed, perhaps in conjunction with your marketability study.

With the risks and mitigations identified for your project, you have planned and structured a project that should be very attractive to all of your constituencies. That is, if you perform a marketability study showing that the project could and should be built, formed a benefit analysis that shows that all of your constituencies will benefit from your proposed project, and you've identified and mitigated the rest of your proposed project, you have a very compelling argument for people to approve or invest in your proposed project.

GUARANTEES

When arranging financing for your project, banks typically require personal guarantees to provide additional support to their lending. As the words imply, a personal guarantee, if exercised by a bank, will access the personal assets of the developer. A project is considered recourse if guarantees are present. A project is considered non-recourse if no guarantees are present. There are three general guarantees that you might encounter. If you are seeking a construction loan, more than likely you will have to provide a construction completion guarantee that you will build the building, build it on time, and build it on budget.

The second type of guarantee you might have to provide the bank is a brief payment guarantee: a guarantee of repayment of the outstanding principal when the loan matures. If a developer structures a loan properly and has a project with strong cash flows, a repayment guarantee is practically without consequence to the developer because the project should be able to service the debt.

The third type of guarantee you might have to provide the bank is a debt service guarantee, that is, a promise that you will pay the bank interest and/or principal when it comes due, that is, monthly. If your early project cash flows are relatively small, a debt service guarantee could be a significant financial burden.

Personal guarantees are a contract that as long as the elements are present, any terms or specific conditions can be negotiated between you and the bank. One structural effect of either a repayment or a debt service guarantee is performance objectives. Should the performance objectives be met, the guarantee would fall away and be of no effect. A performance objective could be minimum debt service coverage that if maintained for a period of time would allow the guarantee to expire. A project is considered partial recourse if guarantees exist but then expire given certain circumstances. Structuring your guarantees to expire is very important because for any subsequent loans you try to pursue, the bank will evaluate your outstanding guarantees, otherwise known as contingent liabilities. If you have too many personal guarantees outstanding, the next lender for your next project may deny your request because you do not appear to have the financial capacity for any additional guarantees should the existing guarantees be exercised by a bank.

LEARNING POINTS FROM THIS CHAPTER

After reading this chapter, I should:

- Understand the typical line items included in a development budget and operating pro forma.
- Know the ratios banks and investors commonly use to measure a property's performance and/or evaluate a property for a loan.
- Know how an investor is motivated to pursue or not pursue a project.
- Understand the purposes of a feasibility study and its essential components.
- Know the different types of personal guarantees.

CHAPTER 11

Contractors, Consultants, and Construction Contracts

A s before, it is not within the scope of this book to offer a comprehensive discussion of contractors and construction contracts, so this chapter, like others in this book, addresses the chapter topic from the perspective of the developer; that is, how does a developer use and interpret the information as it is being created or interpret the information after it has been created?

BUDGETING AND SCHEDULING

In the last chapter, we talked about gathering information to pull together a budget. I am beginning this chapter by talking about some of the nonquantitative factors that affect project costs (budgets). The first of these nonquantitative factors is the experience or relative lack of experience of the project team. An inexperienced developer is typically not as efficient as an experienced developer on account of lack of experience. For this reason alone, a project done by an inexperienced developer, everything else being equal, will cost more than the same project done by an experienced developer. The reason for this additional cost is nothing more than the lack of experience or the ability to obtain cost savings from volume purchasing of materials and labor. Does this mean an inexperienced developer should stop now because he or she is uncompetitive due to a higher project cost? No. Everyone has to start somewhere. Just understand that an inexperienced developer will face an additional challenge that will have to be mitigated. In time, the inexperienced developer will become experienced and this challenge will diminish.

A second nonquantitative factor is how much the scope of your project coincides with the project programming and design. The differences between your project and your budget line items and size can vary for any number of reasons, including choice of materials or the property type. Everything else being equal, a residential building is more expensive than an office building because of the number of additional features (kitchens and bathrooms) that must be constructed for an apartment building as opposed to an office building. Does this mean that you should not build residential buildings? No, you should just understand that a residential building is more expensive than an office building. Location has a significant effect on your budget, whether you are building in a city or in a rural environment. Both have restrictions in terms of access and delivery of materials, for example. Location obviously also has an effect because of weather conditions; you might have to budget additional monies to compensate for weather conditions such as snow in the Northeast as opposed to hurricanes in the Southeast. A fourth nonquantitative factor that affects your developed budget is the budget definition, that is, having adequately detailed budget line items to manage aspects of the development process adequately. Many beginning developers try to summarize budget categories to save themselves time, but they learn quickly that once construction has started, there is not enough information to manage the project properly and cost overruns result. Scheduling of the project also has a major effect on cost. As with location, you have to budget for anticipated weather conditions during construction, typically adding more time to the schedule. Effects of scheduling also include the choice of using normal or conventional scheduling, where processes follow each other on a sequential basis, as opposed to fast-track scheduling, where project processes overlap to save time in the overall construction period.

CONTRACTORS AND CONSTRUCTION CONTRACTS

I have to offer a caveat before describing the different contractors: I'm going to describe the typical categories, but there are so many different permutations in the market today that the pure definitions generally no longer apply. Additional legal requirements vary based on location, so it is advisable to seek legal counsel as appropriate. That being said, the first category of contractors is an owner-builder.

And owner-builder can be either a real estate developer or a sponsor-builder. As a real estate developer, a contractor often finds simple projects such as a warehouse or a distribution center being requested by a client. The contractor can find a site and then build the project. It is not the contractor's main business, but the situation is such that a warehouse or a distribution center is a fairly simple construction project. Thus, the contractor acts as a real estate developer. A contractor acting as a sponsor-builder builds turnkey projects for clients like McDonald's, Kohl's Department Store, and Sears, which have a variety of fixed plans for different store themes. The client locates and obtains a site and has a full set of vetted plans to give to the contractor. The contractor is responsible for obtaining construction financing and then builds the building according to the plans given by the client. Once the construction is complete, the client pays an amount to the contractor representing the cost of construction, including any interest and fees on the loan, plus a fee.

A general contractor is a contractor who takes sole responsibility for constructing a project. In many ways, a general contractor acts like a broker by locating and arranging for a variety of subcontractors to do various trade work. A subcontractor is a contractor who does specific types of work such as electrical, plumbing, or steel. The general contractor, after arranging all of the subcontractors, is paid a fee for the coordination efforts.

Another category of contractor is a construction manager. There are two types of construction managers, defined by the responsibilities they have for a project. In general, a construction manager is responsible for coordinating the construction effort and acting as an agent of the owner or developer. The first type of construction manager is not much different than a general contractor. This construction manager locates, coordinates and signs contracts with all of the subcontractors but also acts as a consultant to the owner regarding various construction matters, including the review change orders. This type of construction manager is referred to as a construction manager at risk. The second type of construction manager is a construction manager as consultant. A construction manager as consultant merely acts as an agent of the owner and coordinates the construction effort between the owner and the general contractor. A construction manager as consultant does not sign contracts with subcontractors; the owner signs contracts with subcontractors.

There are a number of reasons for you to use or not use a construction manager. However, in today's world, because of the complexity of construction, and the many other things you as a developer have to spend your time on, you are often well advised to hire a construction manager, whether a construction manager at risk or a consultant. The construction manager gets paid a fee for the effort, and that fee, of course, is part of the overall development project cost.

RISK MANAGEMENT DURING CONSTRUCTION

If you start to think about the construction contract, you should understand that it is the concept of risk allocation via contract. When negotiating the construction contract, the three parties—the owner, the architect, and the contractor—all have specific responsibilities under the contract. The owner, for example, is responsible for providing adequate project funding and paying the contractor the amount due. The owner is responsible for providing a site ready for construction and construction documents (the construction drawings and specifications) sufficient for the efficient and expeditious completion of the contractor's work. While these points may seem obvious, they are not; they have to be detailed in the construction contract. If the owner does not, say, have the site ready for construction, this situation could delay the project, sometimes significantly. Not having the site ready for construction could mean not having yet acquired the property or not having received the necessary entitlements for the construction work to begin.

The architect is responsible for the complete design of the building, including whether the drawings meet all of the relevant building codes and other regulatory requirements. The architect is responsible for all design errors and omissions as well. A key point to mention here is that when deciding on an architect to work on your project, you should require the architect to have errors and omissions insurance to cover the cost of any mistakes.

The contractor is responsible for performing the work in accordance with the contract documents, as well as for completing the work for the amount contracted and within the scheduled time. Once again, these may seem like simple and obvious points, but these points have to be detailed in the construction contract. In addition, the contractor is responsible for making timely payments to the subcontractors. It often happens that general contractors receive payment from the owner but withhold payment to the subcontractors because they are having financial difficulties or are trying to use the monies on other projects. The result of withholding payment, of course, is that the subcontractors may stop work and thus cause significant schedule delays and/or cost overruns.

> _"Education is the progressive discovery of our own ignorance."_
> —Will Durant, philosopher, historian and writer

These are some of the risks to consider as you prepare to draft a request for proposal to send to prospective contractors. We will talk about risk management again under the category of construction management.

PREPARING FOR CONSTRUCTION:
BID PROPOSALS AND REVIEW

One key aspect while you prepare for a request for proposal (RFP) to contractors is to qualify the contractors that you will be soliciting to bid on your project. You generally need to determine their financial and physical wherewithal to complete the project you have planned. The contractor often has to prepurchase some amount of materials or labor before being paid by the owner. Does the contractor have the financial resources to do this? Does the contractor have access to physical resources such as equipment or a qualified labor pool? You may decide to go with an open or closed bidding process. In an open bidding process, you send the RFP to anyone who might be interested, for example, via an advertisement in the newspaper. Using this process, you will not know who the contractors will be who respond to your advertisement, and as a result you accept a fairly large burden in qualifying the various contractors who respond. In the closed bidding process, you prequalify specific contractors and send your RFP only to those specific prequalified contractors. Obviously in a closed bidding process, the burden of prequalifying contractors has been done before the RFP is issued.

Among other things, your RFP details any specific requirements regarding the project that you would like to have a contractor address. These specific requirements could range from qualifications and experience to specific activities. Your RFP will include voluminous documents: the partially completed construction drawings plus the plans and specifications for the project. A specific requirement that you will want to include in your RFP is the RFP response or submission format. The RFP response from contractors is quite lengthy and in some cases sizeable. If you have several contractors responding to your RFP and all of them submit their responses in their own desired format, it will be virtually impossible for you to compare responses on an equivalent basis. So your RFP should specify a particular submission format to be used by the responding contractors that details which line items should be shown, including the various column categorizations, subtotals, and the like. More important, you should specify in your RFP that any contractor who does not submit a response in your required format will have that response automatically rejected.

Preparing an RFP correctly should take a significant amount of time. Of course, the detail and volume of the RFP vary, based on the size of the project, but it is not unusual for the preparation of an RFP to take several weeks if not months for very large projects.

After an RFP is issued, whether through an open or closed bidding process, it is not unusual to convene a meeting in which the interested contractors gather and you review the details of your RFP. Questions may be asked and answered at this time, including a visit to the project site if possible and practical. Occasionally questions arise that are relevant and important and perhaps clarify certain matters that were unclear in the RFP. If such occurs, then you might issue RFP addenda. The addenda become official documents and part of the original RFP.

When you have received several responses to your RFP, you need to review them for matters such as their exclusions and exceptions. Just like the footnotes to a financial statement, the exclusions and exceptions should be read first, before you read the various numbers in the response. The reason for this, of course, is that the exclusions and exceptions outline the parameters by which the numbers were prepared. The next obvious action should be to literally take a calculator and add up every number in the RFP responses to verify that the subtotals and totals are correct. Along with this math check, you should also evaluate the correctness of the calculation for the contractor's markup.

We earlier said that the preparation of an RFP could take several weeks. Similarly, the review of the various RFP responses could take an additional several weeks to perform. I mention the time involved so that you can appreciate how much must be fit into the development schedule to allow for this work to be done.

CONSTRUCTION DOCUMENTS AND CONSTRUCTION AGREEMENTS

After reviewing the RFP responses and awarding a contract to a particular contractor, you now work on gathering, negotiating and preparing the construction documents. The construction documents include the contract agreement, construction drawings, plans and specifications, site plan, and soil borings; in essence, you include any document that is relevant to the construction process and take the attitude of transparency by providing the contractor with all relevant documents so the contractor cannot later claim to have been unaware of a material fact.

You may have noticed that when I was discussing the RFP, I often used words that sounded legalistic. While an RFP is not technically a legal agreement, it contains elements of what defines a legal contract, that is, the RFP being issued is an offer, and the RFP response is an acceptance. If an RFP is issued and responded to, the owner cannot rescind the RFP without cause and with a right to rescind clearly stated in the original RFP. The contractor's preparation of an RFP is time-consuming and costly. As a result an RFP response is not made casually. A key recommendation for the contract agreement is to attach the original RFP and the RFP response as exhibits to the construction contract. Doing so ensures that the RFP and RFP response are made legal documents and thus can be referred to if there should be any disputes during construction.

Let's now outline the different types of construction agreements. My caveat mentioned earlier regarding the standard definitions of contractors also applies to construction agreements. The following are the standard definitions, but through time, the standard definitions have been more general and often combine elements of different types of the standard form agreements. Be sure you completely understand the precise terms and conditions of a construction contract.

The first common type of contract is a lump sum contract that states one amount for the completion of a project. Many developers are naive about the reality of a lump sum contract. If you recall, when you issued an RFP, your construction drawings very likely were less than 100 percent complete. As such, the contractor honestly provided you with a single amount or lump sum for the completion of the project, basing that amount on construction drawings that were less than 100 percent complete. Any changes made to finalize the construction drawings or any substantive change orders that occur during construction will modify (and probably increase) the amount of the lump sum contract. So do not succumb to the belief that the amount of a lump sum contract is a guaranteed amount for the construction.

A cost-plus fixed fee or a cost-plus percentage fee contract means that the owner will pay for the actual material and labor costs, plus the contractor's fixed amount or percentage fee. Needless to say, a cost-plus percentage fee contract is the most expensive type of contract because if material and labor costs increase, so does the contractor's fee.

> *"Patience is the companion of wisdom."*
> —St. Augustine

A design-build contract is often used for turnkey projects. Here a contractor has an architect who is preparing the construction drawings while the contractor begins physical construction from the drawings already completed. This system is used to minimize the project risk for an owner and to reduce the construction schedule by overlapping the design phase and construction phase of a project. In other words, the result of the design build contract is that you have a fast-track construction project, meaning that certain construction processes are being done simultaneously or ahead of a complete set of construction drawings. Most construction projects today are design-build or fast-track construction. There is a risk with design-build projects because if changes are subsequently made affecting work already in place, total costs will be higher as a result. However, many developers and contractors believe that this is an acceptable risk, given that they can typically deliver the project to the market sooner than if they used a standard or conventional construction schedule.

Additional aspects that you should be aware of in a construction contract include the term "time is of the essence," which puts the parties on notice to do everything in their capacity to complete the provisions of the contract as soon as possible. This provision becomes particularly important in cases of force majeure. Force majeure is an act of God or something that occurs that was clearly outside the control of all the parties involved. Examples might be a hurricane or other significant weather event. If the phrase "time is of the essence" is included in the contract, a significant weather event does not dismiss the parties from a construction contract; instead, the parties have to do what is necessary to get the work completed as close as possible to the original schedule, although no one is held responsible or penalized for the force majeure event. The parties can be penalized only if they do not act as if time is of the essence.

RISK MANAGEMENT: PART 2

During construction, the risk control techniques that can be used include retainage, which is the concept that a certain percentage of money (often 5 to 20 percent) is withheld from the payment to a contractor to ensure that the contractor satisfactorily completes the work. Another method of controlling risk is the use of performance bonds and insurance. We will talk about this topic a little later in this chapter. You should also be very conscious, if applicable, of union relations. Do not entirely trust a contractor who tells you that his relationship with the union is fine. You should contact the union directly to inquire about the contractor you would like to use; also ask whether there will be a contract negotiation of any kind during your construction period. If one is scheduled, that contract negotiation could delay your project. Accounting and internal financial controls are important as well, as is the use of sophisticated scheduling techniques.

SCHEDULING

Here I outline three of the most common types of schedules used. Project schedules are necessary as a summary plan and as an effective control tool. A schedule is very important for the current project, but it also can be useful as a benchmarking tool for future similar projects.

The simplest type of schedule is a project milestone schedule (see Table 11.1).

A milestone schedule shows where you should be, given certain aspects of the project, and what you have actually achieved. It is not a particularly sophisticated method of scheduling, but it is better than having no schedule.

A bar chart or Gantt chart schedule details specific tasks and then indicates the actual time the task took. There are variations in the way a Gantt chart is laid out, but typically the time schedules for each task are indicated by a dotted line, and when that task is actually started and completed, a solid line is drawn for that task. So it becomes quite clear where you are on a project schedule.

A critical path or critical path method (CPM) schedule leaves out the various paths to be completed—some of which are simultaneous tasks—and visually shows which tasks must be completed before a subsequent task can be started.

The example schedule shown in Figure 11.1 is very simplistic. Typically, a critical path chart involves many, many processes, and I often joke that a critical path chart looks similar to a DNA molecule.

BONDING AND INSURANCE

An essential part of risk management during construction is the use of surety bonds. *Surety bonds* as a term is actually meaningless because it is

TABLE 11.1. Project Milestone Chart

Task	Date Due	Actual
Acquire land	6/1/2008	6/6/2008
Design	7/30/2008	
Bid	8/15/2008	
Financing	9/15/2008	
Construction	9/30/2008	
Completion	5/1/2009	

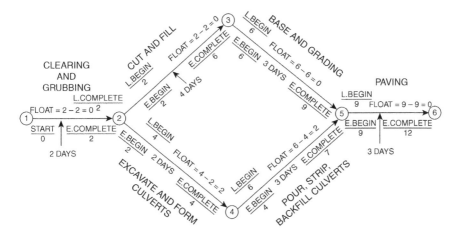

FIGURE 11.1 Critical Path Method Schedule

not specific to the type of bonds actually in place. To say a project has surety bonds is not much different than saying a person has insurance. What kind of insurance? A project has surety bonds? What kind of surety bonds? Surety bonds are a third-party guarantee for the performance of another's obligations.

Surety bonds are present during two stages of the construction process. The first stage is during the precontract stage, when you are working on RFPs. The first type of surety bond during precontract is a bid bond, a bond issued by a surety company that states that the contractor responding to your RFP has the financial and physical wherewithal to do the work specified in the RFP. You specify in your RFP that any contractor who wishes to submit a response to the RFP must also include a bid bond. The cost is borne by the contractor and becomes a sunk cost if the contractor is not awarded the eventual contract. There might be a bid and proposal bond during the precontract stage as well. The bid bond functions the same as I explained earlier. A proposal bond says that should a contractor be selected or awarded the contract for the work, the contractor will participate and begin negotiating a construction contract. It may seem nonsensical that a contractor would not be delighted to receive a contract award, but sometimes a contractor will take on a construction job despite having an RFP response outstanding. As such, that contractor may not be able to work on two projects simultaneously. The problem that you have is that you have spent several weeks or months working on analyzing RFP proposals and now find that the contractor you selected is unavailable, so you must restart the bid review process costing you time and money. A proposal bond would compensate you for that extra cost.

> *"The most successful people are those who are good at Plan B."*
> —James Yorke, mathematician and physics professor

During the contract stage, there are two common types of surety bonds, the first of which is a performance bond. A performance bond states that a contractor will perform all of the duties and hold all of the responsibilities as specified in the construction contract. If the contractor does not do so, you have the right to make a claim to the surety company and thus be reimbursed for the cost of that contractor's nonperformance. Another common bond during the contract stage is a payment bond. A payment bond states that the general contractor will make timely payments to his subcontractors. If a contractor does not, you can make a claim to the surety company to reimburse you for the cost of nonpayment or perhaps replacement of the general contractor or subcontractor(s) involved. These two bonds are often combined into a single bond called a payment and performance bond.

In some circumstances, such as working with the government or outside the United States, the owners may not be willing to accept surety bonds as security. In this case, you require the contractor to issue a letter of credit that effectively takes the place of and would function like a surety bond.

At this point, you will finalize your various project documents, obtain the remaining building permits and municipal approvals, and internally decide whether to proceed with construction. If you refer to the development process chart in the first chapter, we are at the end of the preconstruction phase, and the decision point symbol on the development process chart shown in Chapter 1 changes from a star to a stop sign/green light. The decision to start construction is crucial because once you start construction, you practically cannot stop. A partially completed project does not have value. So you and your team must be convinced that you have planned and arranged the project well enough to confidently proceed with construction. If you decide to proceed, then the shovel goes into the dirt.

Let's put this in perspective: We are now in Chapter 11 of a book describing the development process, and just now, after 11 chapters, we are actually beginning physical construction. So you can appreciate the amount of detailed planning that goes into the development process. And we still have several chapters to go before we complete the discussion on real estate development and investment.

CONSTRUCTION MONITORING: DRAW MEETINGS, MANAGING CHANGE ORDERS

Now that construction has begun, our focus is directed toward monitoring the construction activities. You transition from primarily being a planner to primarily being a manager. As a developer, you are not expected to necessarily be involved in all of the details of the construction phase: That is why you most likely engage a construction manager. However, as a developer you should be aware of major activities such as monthly loan funding requests, problems that can occur, and the closing out of the construction phase.

You should also be aware of what I call the unpleasant surprises. As a developer, surprises are unpleasant because they bring the unexpected, and in development, the unexpected usually means trouble and extra cost. The first unexpected surprise is often associated with delays in the project. Think about what could cause a delay in a construction project. Frankly, just about anything can cause a delay, and delays are far more important than cost overruns.

With regard to cost overruns, many construction loans have a concept called loan balancing. Loan balancing states that should actual cost exceed budgeted cost, the developer is required by the bank to contribute additional equity to the project. This seems like a reasonable requirement, except that the measurement of whether actual cost exceeds budgeted cost is done on a prospective basis. The bank has the right to call loan balancing at any time, based on its projections of cost to complete compared with the budget (cost to complete is actual money spent to date plus costs expected to complete the project). Loan balancing becomes a major point of discussion between the borrower and the bank. Whenever a bank calls loan balancing, it has the right to stop funding its construction loan until the required equity is contributed to the project. Usually the time given to raise equity after a bank calls loan balancing is about 30 days, or the time between loan draws. Given what I've just said, you should always be preparing a cost-to-complete budget so that you are never caught by surprise when a bank calls loan balancing on your project.

Another common surprise is leases that cancel or fall through (are not executed after discussions and negotiation) on your project. You may have a project, for example, that you think has a substantial preleasing level; however, because of the economic conditions of the prospective tenants or the macroeconomy, tenants may have the right to cancel their lease commitment. Needless to say, if this should happen, your project more than likely will suffer additional costs due to increased leasing costs and possibly increased tenant improvement expenses. With these additional costs, loan balancing may be called by the bank. So you have the idea that cash equity calls through loan balancing requirements, or leases canceling, sometimes as a result of delays, are some rather unpleasant surprises that plague developers. I mention these three common unpleasant surprises because they are common. They could happen to you, so be prepared and aware of these problems ahead of time.

Other common construction problems include inaccurate project financial records and reports, excessive change order costs, government compliance issues, insufficient staffing, project communication breakdowns, and uninsured property and casualty losses. Any of these problems could result in the unpleasant surprises I mentioned earlier, so you should be aware and diligent.

A key aspect of managing your project during the construction phase involves some basic common sense, such as clarity when defining responsibility for various tasks. You should establish an effective contract administration team charged with managing all of the contracts on a construction project. When managing contracts, the contract administration team assures that terms agreed to in the contracts are actually being performed. I suppose you could say that the contract administration team makes sure that you get what you pay for. The contract administration team is also charged with reviewing the various change orders and other documentation that arise during a project.

While there will be meetings regarding the construction progress daily and weekly, I want to now focus on the monthly construction meetings, because these meetings lead to the monthly loan draw. In this meeting, everything is discussed about the project, including construction status, cost to complete budget, potential change orders, and schedule status. All relevant participants are included in the meeting: the contractor, subcontractors, owner's representatives, bank representative, and perhaps even the building department. These meetings can last from a few hours to an entire day, depending on the size of the project and the number of issues that need to be discussed. Each of these meetings starts with the contractor's schedule of values, which is the contractor's list of all budgeted expenses relative to costs to complete and amounts billed on the project. All the participants at the monthly meeting review the schedule of values to agree upon the point that work claimed to be done by the contractor is in fact completed and thus the contractor is due to be paid. Any adjustments to the contractor's schedule of values agreed upon at the monthly meeting are noted, and the contractor incorporates those changes and reissues the schedule of values to the developer after the conclusion of the monthly meeting.

Now the developer prepares the draw package for the bank by taking the contractor's revised schedule of values and adding to it invoices from the architect, engineer, as well as including marketing expenses, brokerage fees, loan interest, developer's fee, and other costs. The draw package format that is submitted to a bank for the monthly loan draw will vary but includes all of these invoices plus partial lien waivers and any other supporting documentation necessary to satisfy the bank that expenses are legitimate and should be funded from the construction loan that month.

A key activity during the construction process is managing change orders. It is naive to believe that any project will not have a change order; there will always be change orders, no matter how much you plan your project. Changes will always occur; the goal is to keep them as few in number as possible. Change orders are reviewed by the project architect and, if applicable, the construction manager before reaching the owner for approval. This is one instance where the contract administration team will play a significant role. The review of change orders is important because the developer typically does not have the right to approve a change order without also obtaining the bank's consent. The bank's consent is necessary because the bank is concerned about monitoring actual costs and looking for possible instances of loan balancing problems. There are a couple of ways of managing change orders. When receiving a change order, you should do a thorough cost analysis to ensure that unit costs are reasonable and within ranges established in the construction contract and in the market. This analysis should also include a basic math check to see if the various numbers on the change order add up correctly. Another common way of managing change orders is by establishing a minimum dollar amount in the construction contract simply to reduce the number of change orders. That is, that a contractor cannot issue a change order unless it exceeds a minimum dollar amount. If too many change orders are issued, for, say, nominal amounts, the volume of paperwork will overwhelm the contract administration team and inevitably work on the problem will slow down as a result of slow approvals for work to be done.

The review of change orders should also include an assessment of the reason for the change order, as well as who issued the change order. It is not uncommon that one particular segment of a project may generate an inordinate amount of change orders, as compared with the rest of the project. This could be because of an incompetent or inexperienced subcontractor or perhaps unclear drawings by the architect. In either case, a concentration of change orders in particular areas of a project indicates a weakness in the project that should be investigated. The contract administration team typically maintains a log of these change orders that includes the issuer name, reasoning behind the change order, the amount, and whether the change order was actually approved by the owner. This log of change orders can also be used for future projects to benchmark potential problem areas.

> *"Trust, but verify."*
> —Ronald Reagan

Other construction phase problems may come up as well. It is not unusual that two subcontractors worked together on another project and had a disagreement that carries forward into your project. You should make the necessary inquiries on a regular basis to ensure that this interpersonal antagonism does not happen because if it does, the disagreements can potentially slow down work on your project and cause you a variety of problems. You should also be aware of potential illegalities, such as construction workers stealing materials; a strong inventory control system would be a possible solution for this. Also be always aware of public perceptions regarding your project. If the public perceives, for whatever reason, that your project is significantly behind schedule (whatever that means) or has some sort of difficulty, that perception could extend into the leasing market and perhaps dissuade potential tenants from considering your building thus causing you future difficulties. A common solution for erroneous public perceptions is issuing regular press releases describing current activities on the project, so there is no misperception about construction.

TENANT IMPROVEMENTS AND COORDINATION

As you finish the project base building construction, you change your focus on to tenant improvements and tenant coordination efforts. As you speak to prospective tenants, they first will be interested in what work can be done to improve the space they intend to lease (for their needs), while you will be concerned about coordinating those activities with the remaining base building work still going on. The work that's done within a prospective tenant's space is described in a document called a work letter. The work letter is attached to the lease as an exhibit. The work letter goes into complete detail as to the work that will be done within a prospective tenant's space, including who the contractor and architect will be among other details. The work letter also addresses who will pay for the cost of these tenant improvements.

When the base building work is budgeted for a project, a certain standard building finish cost is included. The base building contractor who constructs the building will not necessarily install the standard tenant improvements at the same time the base building construction occurs because a prospective tenant may decide against standard finishes and want to substitute alternative finishes. These substitutions or credits will be detailed in the work letter. Perhaps the tenant wants extensive work done within the space that is considered above standard work (such as types of material used or features included within the space). The above standard work would be a cost to that prospective tenant. As a leasing incentive, you might provide what's called a tenant allowance to the prospective tenant thus sharing the costs of the above standard tenant improvements. For example, if the standard work is US$150 per square foot, you might decide, in order to entice the tenant to sign a lease, to give a 50 percent tenant allowance or pay half the cost of the above-standard work. Whatever you agree to do would be detailed in the work letter agreements and should also be reflected in your overall development budget; that is, if you give an improvement allowance to a tenant, its cost comes as an additional cost to your project. Note: the giving of additional (beyond the budgeted amounts) tenant allowances in a difficult leasing market is often a circumstance giving a bank the rationale to call loan balancing.

Another coordination effort that has to be considered is that now you will have multiple contractors working on your project site, not only your base building contractor but also any tenant improvement contractors. There is always some controversy regarding where the workers park their cars or when they can use the building elevator to access the space. Contractor coordination is incredibly important because many leases include deadline dates for the tenant improvement work to be completed. If the tenant improvement work is not completed on time due to your delay or prevention of the tenant's contractors' access to this site, the tenant may have the right to cancel the lease.

CONSTRUCTION CLOSEOUT

Several activities occur as you complete construction and work toward closing out the construction contracts. Punch list items either need to be corrected or are still to be completed. The punch list is part of the construction contract, thus all parties—that is, the contractor and owner's representatives—must agree that there are items to be corrected or to be completed before those items can be entered on the punch list. The contractor cannot be released from the contract until all items on the punch list are satisfactorily completed.

You should also begin to assemble and then verify final lien waivers from the contractor, subcontractors, and anyone else who did work on the project. The lien waivers are legal documents signed by the respective contractors waiving their rights to place a mechanic's lien on your property because they assert that they have received all payment for work they have done. These lien waivers are important in terms of future sale of the building or refinancing, thus collection of final lien waivers is essential.

Finally, the building and all systems should be started and tested. Any warranties, maintenance manuals, test reports, and the like should be collected because they are necessary for making any future claims on the original manufacturers. Bills for sale have to be collected for any personal property such as desk chairs and the like installed in your building.

Only when you are fully satisfied with the work that's been completed and have received all the necessary documentation are you in a position to release the contractor from the contract and release any retained payments withheld.

LEARNING POINTS FROM THIS CHAPTER

After reading this chapter, I should:

- Understand nonquantitative issues that affect a development budget.
- Know the different types of construction contracts and the role of a construction manager.
- Know the different types of risk-management techniques during construction, including the use of insurance and surety bonds.
- Appreciate the responsibilities of a contract administration team.
- Understand what occurs during a monthly draw meeting and how it leads to a construction loan draw from the bank.
- Have a basic understanding of tenant improvement work and what occurs during the closeout of construction activities.

CHAPTER 12

Leases and How They Are Used

As before, it is not within the scope of this book to offer a primer on leases, so this chapter, like others in this book, addresses the chapter topic from the perspective of the developer; that is, how does a developer use and interpret the information as it is being created or interpret the information after it has been created?

VALUE CREATION

With all due respect to appraisers, buildings have no value. Yes, a building structure does have some residual value in the bricks, steel, and concrete, but the building itself is essentially worthless. The true value of any building is in the leases. The leases produce a cash flow annuity, and that annuity is what creates value. It is essential for a developer to focus on the *quality* of the cash flow. As a concept, consider a stock portfolio that has dividends. Each investment has risk, and as you manage a stock portfolio, you are concerned about concentrations and diversification. A building is no different; a building is nothing more than a lease portfolio. Each lease has cash flow, each tenant has a level of risk, and you want to control concentration to ensure diversification in your portfolio (of leases). If you focus on the concept that a building is nothing more than a portfolio of leases, you will have a good understanding of property investment analysis and understand how to evaluate and structure leases. It is the leases in a building that create the value of a building.

WHAT IS A LEASE?

Basically, a lease is a contract between a landlord and a tenant, and if you recall, a contract requires only an offer, acceptance, and consideration—everything else is negotiable. Accordingly, as long as a lease has the essential elements of a contract, everything else is negotiable; there is no such thing as a boilerplate lease. A lease contract limits the common law rights granted to a leasehold in law. Not unlike a fee simple ownership interest, a leasehold interest is a bundle of rights. Both a fee simple ownership interest and a leasehold interest have the right of possession and the right of quiet enjoyment. A leasehold, on the other hand, *may have* the right of modification and may have the right of sale or assignment. The details of these two rights are some of the major items negotiated in a lease contract.

COMMON LEASE STRUCTURES

Broad categories of leases include a gross lease and a net lease. In a gross lease, the tenant pays an amount to the property owner that includes a base rent plus an (estimated) amount to reimburse various operating expenses. A net lease, on the other hand, is a base rent plus charges for a share of various actual expenses incurred by the property owner. Note: You should be careful when reading and evaluating a net lease. Today, most people who refer to a net lease are really referring to a triple net lease, and there are actually a single net lease and a double net lease as well. In a triple net lease, a tenant pays a share of real estate taxes, insurance, and common area maintenance expenses. In a double net lease, a tenant pays a share of real estate taxes and insurance, and in a single net lease, a tenant only pays a share of real estate taxes. To determine what kind of lease you might be evaluating, refer to the section of the lease that addresses cost reimbursement or allocation of expenses, but be sure to read the lease in its entirety.

> *"More and more investors are looking at investing in real estate as if they were investing in bonds. When they look at a shopping center, they see a mini-mutual fund of companies [in the tenants]."*
> —Rob Hanna, CB Richard Ellis, CBRE World Conference, September 9, 2004

There are several general categories of leases. The first category of lease is a graduated lease, which is nothing more than a lease where its base rent increases at some specified rate over the term of the lease. In a stairstep lease, the base rent is fixed for a period of time, and then it increases by some specified rate and is again fixed for a similar period of time. An index lease is a graduated lease where the base rent increases on the basis of changes in a predetermined index, such as the Consumer Price Index or CPI. (If the year-to-year CPI increases by 3 percent, the base rent amount then increases by 3 percent.) With a fixed lease, the base rent is fixed for the entire term of the lease. (The most common type of fixed lease is an apartment rental lease.) A reappraisal lease is commonly associated with a ground or land lease. Ground lease rent is based on the current value of the land at the time the lease is signed. The value of the land will likely increase over the term of the lease, which in the United States is the term is often 99 years. So to better reflect the value of the land in the ground lease payment, the land may be reappraised at, say, every 25 years of the ground lease term and the rent adjusted by the same percentage that the land value increased. A percentage lease typically applies to a retail tenant. A retail tenant on a percentage lease pays a lower base rent but also pays a specified percentage of its sales (as defined in the lease) as additional rent.

If you reflect upon some of the definitions of the types of leases, you will begin to understand that the lease contract is actually an exercise in economics. You are trying to structure a lease, including the rent payments, such that during the term of the lease the property owner makes a regular profit that is not reduced by increased expenses and provides adequate debt coverage to satisfy the lenders. The best example of this is choosing a gross lease over a triple net lease. Again, with a gross lease, the tenant pays one amount that covers a base rent plus a presumed allocation of expenses over the term of the lease. Let's say that the lease term is five years. How confident do you feel deciding on rental amounts that will match or be higher than the rate of inflation for your operating expenses over the next five years? This is the dilemma faced on every lease transaction; leases are an exercise in economics and economic forecasting.

As you consider the expenses you want to charge a tenant in a lease, you also need to consider how the rent will be calculated. Will the (graduated lease) rent be adjusted on annual basis? When the rent adjustment occurs, does the rent adjustment occur from a mathematical perspective at the beginning of the month or at the end of the month? These points could significantly affect the cash flows and yield of a particular lease contract and on the value of your (building) lease portfolio.

When you are structuring the expense pass-through to a tenant in a lease, it is not unusual to structure an expense stop (that is, a maximum annual expense pass-through amount) or an expense base, according to which the property owner cannot pass-through expenses until the expenses exceed a predetermined amount. Again, the decisions made regarding rent escalations and expense pass-throughs have a direct economic effect on a particular lease contract and the value of your (building) lease portfolio.

What types of concessions might you give a tenant? Common concessions like a period of free rent or renewal options come at a cost to the property owner. Any concessions given to a tenant should correspond with a concession given to the landlord by the tenant. Concessions vary greatly and could include equity participation, right of first refusal, and relocation options; they are not necessarily monetary in nature. The type and amount of concessions given to a tenant depend wholly on market supply-and-demand conditions and the intensity of the property owner's desire to obtain a particular tenant.

All of the terms of the lease, whether financial or legal, establish the value of a property or add to the property's cost base. Nevertheless, remember that a building is no more than a portfolio of leases.

LEASE MANAGEMENT AND ANALYSIS

A key part of lease management includes regularly reviewing your lease plan for the size of spaces leased. You want to be sure that tenants are effectively placed within the building so that there are few odd–shaped or small leftover spaces that cannot be leased, making them non-revenue-producing and thus reducing the overall value of your building. Given the placement of tenants within a building, do not overlook the value of an effective tenant mix, balancing national tenants and local tenants, as well as tenants of different industries. This balance of tenants also extends to the lease maturities and options in their leases. In a new building, if you were to execute leases with a common maturity of five years, in five years your building could be vacant because all of the leases expired. So when evaluating leases, you should consider staggering the lease maturities as much as you possibly can so that at any given point in time, you have enough leases in place to provide, say, a minimum debt service coverage for the building. The staggering of lease maturities is not an easy task, but it is not impossible either. If you effectively stagger the lease maturities so that your building consistently has a minimum debt service coverage, and have reliable credit tenants, you can have a building cash flow that will sustain itself during downturns in the real estate cycle.

In addition, a database of lease abstracts should be established for all of the leases within a building. A lease abstract is a detailed summary of the terms and conditions of a particular lease. The idea behind the lease abstract is that it saves you the time of repeatedly reading a lease contract; however, leases have become so complicated in their terms that the lease abstract can be almost as lengthy as the lease contract itself.

> *"Pick battles big enough to matter, small enough to win."*
> —Jonathan Kozol, American nonfiction writer and educator

Each pending or proposed lease should be subjected to a thorough financial analysis that assesses the rent to be paid over the term of the lease, plus the value of any concessions given. One way to do this financial analysis and compare one lease to another is to prepare a calculation of what's called effective rent. Effective rent is the actual rent spread over the life of the lease to be achieved by you, the landlord, after deducting the value of concessions from the base rate. Calculating a lease's effective rent allows you to compare disparate leases and bring the value of them to a common level. An effective rent calculation uses present value techniques applied to the cash inflows and outflows of a lease.

Calculating effective rent is a straightforward process. First, schedule the rents, escalations, and pass-through expenses from a lease over the term of the lease. Then schedule any cash outflows from the lease (which might include free rent or tenant improvement allowances, for example) to arrive at a net annual rent number. Using the net rent number for each year, calculate three figures:

1. An average rent per square foot.
2. The net present value rent per square foot.
3. The effective rent.

The average rent per square foot generally is not that important, but it is required to be reported in audited financial statements. The net present value of rent per square foot is a useful statistic. It provides the value of a lease. With the value of a lease—if allowed per the contract—you can sell the lease to an (third-party) investor. Many net lease transactions are based on this concept of monetizing a lease. The effective rent uses the net present value rent per square foot and multiples it by the present value of $1 (using the term of the lease as the period). The effective rent brings the net present value rent (over the term of the lease) to an annual present value basis.

Doing an effective rent calculation allows you to compare differently structured leases. As you complete your financial analysis to the point that you are satisfied with the yield generated by a particular lease, you should then incorporate that particular lease and its financial terms into your overall property financial pro forma to see what the effect of the addition of a particular lease has on the overall building or lease portfolio. When you consider the amount of analysis that must occur for an individual lease, consider how much work must be devoted to analyzing leases for a building that perhaps has dozens or even hundreds of leases. It is a lot of work.

LEARNING POINTS FROM THIS CHAPTER

After reading this chapter, I should:

- Know some of the different types of leases.
- Appreciate the lease portfolio concept.
- Understand that lease terms reflect an exercise in economics.
- Understand some lease management methods.

CHAPTER 13

Marketing Focus of Development

It may seem unusual to have a discussion about marketing this late in a book about development. At this point in the book, you probably appreciate that virtually everything you do as a developer involves marketing. Had I introduced the concept of marketing in the first chapter, as you will see after reading this chapter, there would have been many concepts that you would not have learned about yet.

Marketing is a fully involved process (Figure 13.1), beginning with market research. Starting the process of market research usually results in a market study report, and after completing a market study, you should prepare your marketability study. Following the marketability study, you would be able to prepare your financial feasibility study. Then, because you have the numbers available, you can easily prepare an appraisal or valuation of a project. All of these activities are interconnected. You cannot do one or just a couple of these activities and have a complete marketing effort.

KNOW YOUR TARGET AUDIENCE

A key part of starting your marketing effort is to identify your target audience, but really, you would have done so as you started your market study and worked on your marketability study. Your target audience again is your five constituencies: the government, the community, the investors, the end users (including clients and employees of the end users), and you, the developer.

Marketing is contacting—speaking to your constituencies. First, you analyze the market, then you need to persuade the users that their needs are met, package your product (the building) and assist your target market to ensure they know about your product, and follow up on their expectations of satisfaction. Let's look at a couple of the steps, particularly persuading users that their needs are met. What does it mean to persuade the users?

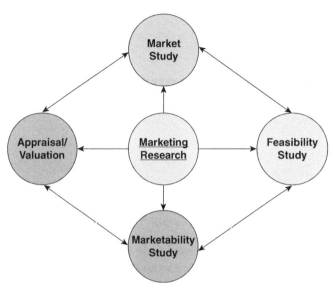

FIGURE 13.1   Marketing Activity Circle

Once again, in development we are talking about a constant marketing and sales effort. When someone from your constituency outlines needs, it is up to you to not only meet those needs but also persuade or show the constituency that their needs are met. This persuasion occurs through the marketing effort, which provides information to the constituency showing that their needs would be met by a particular product. A second important part of marketing is to follow up on expectations of satisfaction. At what point do you follow up? Follow-up occurs from the moment you start to speak with a particular constituency—no later.

Overall, marketing is about what to do and when to do it. Marketing examines the timing for planning and implementing marketing actions and the activities relative to the various steps in the development process. This is why marketing is so important in development and, as I mentioned earlier in this chapter, could have been addressed at the very beginning of this book.

There are three components of marketing: advertising, promotion, and publicity. The advertising provides a static message; that is, advertising identifies an event and indicate its location, date, and time. Advertising can occur verbally (in person or on the radio or television) or in writing. Promotion highlights a particular event or product, but is defined by some sort of activity (for example, giving away balloons to children so parents go to a store that is trying to promote a sale). Publicity is characterized by third-party reporting, such as an article in the newspaper mentioning an event or product. All three—advertising, promotion, and publicity—are components of marketing.

Marketing can be characterized by either shotgun marketing or target marketing. Shotgun marketing, at its name suggests, is broad. It is used when a project design is generic, when the project is designed to appeal to many submarkets, or when there is a vibrant market, and property, space, or units rent or sell quickly. Target marketing, as its name suggests, is marketing to the specific target market you defined when doing your market and marketability studies. You would clearly use target marketing when your project has a unique design meant to appeal to a specific market group, when there is limited market demand for the project, or when the market is just slow in general. Which type of marketing approach should you use for your project? The answer is both! You certainly would not waste your previous effort and ignore your target market. But you should also do shotgun marketing. No one will ever be able to perfectly define a target market, and because a market and its needs change on almost a minute-by-minute basis, you should use target marketing to capture those constituencies you did not define in your target market or those whose needs have changed after defining your target market.

> *"You can quote whatever rent you want, that doesn't mean people are going to pay it."*
> —Riis Christensen with Transwestern Commercial Real Estate Services, commenting on new property owners making best-case assumptions to underwrite their acquisitions, in the *Dallas Business Journal*, March 19, 2004

An important concept to understand is market windows. If you recall from the first chapter, I mentioned the importance of universal knowledge. The concept of market windows is what I referred to when I mentioned universal knowledge. Market windows are changes in the financial cycle, changes in the regulatory cycle, or changes in the economic cycle. When thinking about market windows, you are trying to discern when your project must be accelerated to avoid the perhaps negative effects on your project as a market window closes. On the other hand, a change in the market window could offer an opportunity that did not exist previously. Thus, again, you always must be aware of and consider universal knowledge—any information that could provide you with an opportunity or signal a change in your development strategy.

Your awareness of market windows is why you decided to pursue a real estate development in a particular location or of a particular kind. Market windows you perceive may also postpone your activities. Thus, knowing about market windows starts at the very beginning of the development process and continues throughout, even to the point when you eventually sell your project.

YOUR ESSENTIAL VISION

We have all seen the television spots where a spokesperson, in an animated and energetic style, talks about the homes and leisure activities of a proposed project. As you look closely at the image on the television screen, you do not see homes and leisure activities and instead see nothing more than forest or swampland. This is a bit of an exaggeration, but not that much of one. The spokesperson is projecting a vision onto the viewers through the commercial. What is happening? What really is vision? Vision is a promise, a promise of what will be. Think about it. Why could anyone purchase a house or condo based on construction drawings without vision? A fact of real estate is that no one buys or leases real estate; they buy or lease vision. Let me repeat: *No one buys or leases real estate; they buy or lease vision.* This is a very important concept to understand, and this concept extends directly from the marketability study. You formulate and have vision when you have a real estate development idea. You extend your vision by seeking a site to acquire. Your end-users and buyers have vision when they lease space in or purchase your building. Vision is the foundation of everything you do in development.

However, in order to be effective, unlike some of those television spokespeople, your vision must consist of a delivered product, a defensible market segment or spatial monopoly, and a sales and distribution channel that serves your target market. Failure to deliver a product means that your promise—your vision—is not believable. Failure to have a spatial monopoly means that you really do not have a target market, your marketability study is incomplete (or was not done), and you are solely relying on shotgun marketing. Eventually, perhaps unlike the television spokespeople, you have to actually deliver a complete building—otherwise your marketing message is without substance. While you might succeed from time to time, you are also taking a great risk by not establishing a spatial monopoly. And also, many developers' vision fails because the developer could not get the message out to the target market through an appropriate sales distribution channel.

THE IMPORTANCE OF BRANDING

Brands characterize your project, whether that brand consists of a picture, a design, and/or a name. A brand is one tangible part of your vision. Because it is tangible, it is very important to your marketing effort and in many cases the success of your project. A note: Branding of any product in this context is hugely popular in the United States, and it starting to become important outside the United States. Consider the logos of, say, Pepsi-Cola or McDonalds. If anyone sees the round three-color Pepsi-Cola label or the McDonald's yellow arch, the logos are immediately recognized. Similarly, if you have a unique logo associated with your project, that logo will be immediately associated with your project. Like some of the conditions of vision, brands have to be unique, memorable, identified with the target market, and attractive. You should spend time and thought choosing a brand that will represent your building.

> *"Profit is opinion. Cash is fact."*
> —A REIT executive at *The Institutional Real Estate Letter*
> editorial board meeting, February 20, 2003

Logos (resulting from branding) by themselves must be effective, but so should the project names associated with your project. A classic marketing case involving the wrong choice of name for a product involves the Chevrolet Nova car. The Nova was hugely popular in the United States, so the company executives thought that the citizens of Mexico would also be interested in a practical, affordable car and started the marketing effort and production of the Nova car in Mexico. Unfortunately, the Chevrolet executives did not understand a basic cultural or language issue: that "no va" in Spanish means "it doesn't go." Sales of the car were dismal. Try not to make this mistake with your project in a market where the name of your project might have meaning in another language. Of course, having meaning in another language could be an advantage, as long it is positive and planned.

IMAGE, IDENTITY, AND COMMUNICATION

Creating the right image that is attractive to your target market is essential in real estate. You will broadcast your message of vision and branding through advertising, promotion, and publicity. Often one of the most effective methods of marketing is by telling a story. Tell a story about your project—how it was designed, the thinking behind it. Perhaps describe the story of the site you selected. Oftentimes, knowing this history can help you design and select a brand or name for your project, thus tying in your project more to the local community and endearing yourself to them. People like to read or hear stories. Use this to your advantage. For example, I know one developer who has the history of his project's site, however innocuous, on a plaque in the lobbies of his buildings. Visitors to the building frequently stop to read the story and probably remember the building with a story.

> *"The thing always happens that you really believe in; and the belief in a thing makes it."*
> —Frank Lloyd Wright

The Internet has become a wonderful tool for the developer. Marketing on the Internet through a web site for a real estate project is far less expensive than printing high-quality brochures (that many recipients discard) and reaches a broader audience. Along the line of technology is the use of computer graphics and fiber-optic cameras. (Fiber-optic video cameras are often used to do a tour of a project model to give the web site viewer the impression that he or she is walking through a completed project.) This technology is very effective in today's world and the video can be placed on a project's web site. Remember, people do not buy or lease space; they buy or lease the vision.

COMPONENTS OF MARKETING CENTERS

Before we finish the topic of marketing, I need to address the marketing center. For larger projects (you define what *larger* means), you should utilize a marketing center. A marketing center often incorporates mock-ups of the interiors of various aspects of a project, such as a typical office space or a typical retail space, to give potential tenants or buyers a tangible experience of what the proposed project will be like once completed. You should have a separate marketing center for each component of your project; that is, if you have a mixed-use project with office, retail, and residential, you should have three marketing centers. This marketing center could be one large space, but there should be three dedicated areas for each component of the mixed-use project.

> *"Simplicity is genius."*
> —Bill Shankly, former football manager

The marketing center has needs, such as staffing and equipment. Staffing the marketing center requires a receptionist and a broker and perhaps a tenant improvement coordinator, accountant, or a paralegal. While some of the positions would be commission-based and part-time, salaries would have to be paid to some of the staff. The staff in turn needs equipment, such as desks, a table, chairs, telephones, computers, and the like. You also need some print brochures available, along with displayed floor plans and sample boards for building standard finishes. All of these things cost money and should be included in your development budget and added to the cost of your project (consider our discussion of development budgets and the pre-planning necessary).

LEARNING POINTS FROM THIS CHAPTER

After reading this chapter, I should:

- Appreciate the importance of marketing in the real estate development process.
- Understand how vital the definition and implementation of your vision is to your proposed project.
- Understand how important proper branding is to your project.
- Be familiar with how a market center is structured.

CHAPTER 14

Investment Management

It took 13 chapters to do it, but we finally developed a real estate project. Until about the 1980s, this would have ended the process for most developers. Then, the development process was: find a site, build it, lease it, and then sell it. Many developers would have gone on to hire a property manager, but building and leasing a building was the end of the development process. After the 1980s and the deep real estate recession experienced in the United States, the markets changed substantially, and developers realized that they might have to hold on to their projects much longer than planned. They now had an investment that must be managed, and the planning of their development must include a possible long holding period. Recall from the first chapter Figure 1.3, a four-panel chart depicting the development process. Prior to the 1980s, this chart would have had only three panels. I added the fourth panel to include the investment management phase of development. (See Figure 14.1.)

The investment management phase has three functions: property management, asset management, and portfolio management. Decisions of a day-to-day nature are handled by the property manager. I like to say that the property manager has the ground-level view of a property. Decisions involving the physical, financial, or ownership structure of a property—the property strategic decisions—are performed by the asset manager. I like to say that the asset manager has a 5,000-foot view of the property. The asset manager can clearly see and has access to the project but takes an overview position. Decisions involving a number of properties and the strategic decisions of the portfolio are handled by the portfolio manager. The portfolio manager has a 10,000-foot view of the properties. The portfolio manager can distinguish properties but really does not discern any one of them, because the portfolio manager's focus is the overall performance of all the properties and not just one. (See Figure 14.2.)

The portfolio manager, in turn, is responsible to the investor(s). Some would say looking at Figure 14.2 that this is a lot of people (property, asset,

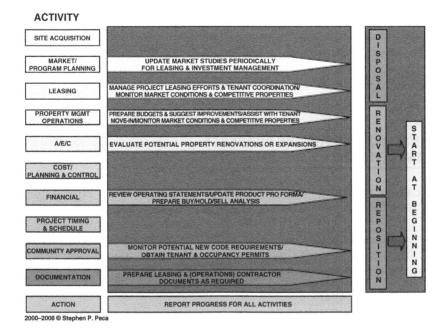

FIGURE 14.1 Development Process—Occupancy and Investment Management Phase

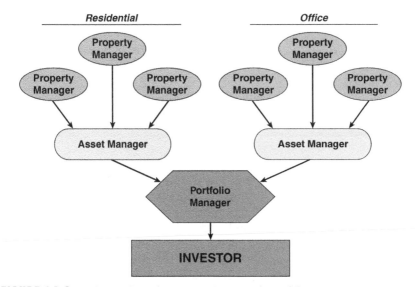

FIGURE 14.2 Relationship of Property, Asset, and Portfolio Managers

and portfolio managers) for a developer who plans to have only one, two, or three properties. It is true that a small developer would not have all of these people, but it should be understood that these functions are distinct and must be effectively performed to have a successful project, whether these functions are done by separate individuals or just one person.

FUNCTION AND GOAL OF PROPERTY MANAGEMENT

The property manager is the person who is responsible for a property on a constant basis. A good definition of a *property manager* is:

> *A profession in which someone other than the owner supervises the operation of a property according to the owner's objectives and consults with the owner on the definition of those objectives and the property's profitability.*

A key aspect of this definition to think about is that the property manager supervises the operation of a property according to the owner's objectives. That is, the property manager is directed by the owner to focus on the property's profitability. The key point is that the property manager's responsibility is to focus on (improve) the property's profitability.

> *"During up times, you see irrational exuberance. In down times, you see irrational depression, so to speak. Reality is probably somewhere in between."*
>
> —J. Brad Smith, principal at Resource Real Estate Partners, in the *Atlanta Business Chronicle*, April 4, 2003

The property manager starts this process by focusing on the property management plan, which outlines how the property is to be managed, with performance benchmarks to improve profitability—in essence, a budget and strategy for managing those things under a property manager's responsibility, such as operating expenses and efficiencies. From the management plan, the property manager prepares the operations manual—the instructions on how the property is physically operated. The property manager also is focused on tenant relations and retention, cash financial recordkeeping, and crisis management. A good property manager also monitors government requirements for both compliance and upcoming changes. Because the property manager is at the property on a daily basis, the property manager is in the best position to attend local government meetings and then learn about or anticipate changes that would affect the property. Also, a good property manager focuses on public relations. I am not referring to tenant relations, but to relations with the community and the local government. As far as most community residents are concerned, the owner of a property is the property manager, who is visible to them. It is important for the property manager to maintain good relations in the community and with the government, so that if you as developer want to do an additional project in the area, your new project will be positively received.

FUNCTION AND GOAL OF ASSET MANAGEMENT

Asset management is a relatively new profession. Prior to the 1980s, institutional investors did not actively invest in commercial real estate. The vast majority of commercial real estate was held by wealthy families and private partnerships (limited partnerships) and managed by a managing equity investor, someone who was intimately involved in the property investments. In the 1980s, institutional investors began perceiving commercial real estate as a diversifier of their investment portfolio. A new breed of third-party asset managers was required to provide expertise to institutional investors taking on, in a fiduciary capacity, the role of managing equity investor, as a result of the lack of real estate knowledge by institutional investors.

An asset manager has a number of important responsibilities, and as a result, particularly in a slower market, asset managers are in high demand by these property owners. Asset managers prepare the property strategic plan. Central to this strategic plan is the buy-sell-hold analysis. The asset manager decides, after performing a detailed financial and market analysis for every property under his or her responsibility, whether to hold on to the property, sell the property, or buy more. The asset manager who decides to hold on to the property often then decides whether the property should be renovated or repositioned, based on the market information received. The asset manager also benchmarks the property managers and, of course, is focused on increasing the property's net income, which leads to its increase in value. If the asset manager decides to buy more properties (or is just starting to acquire holdings), the asset manager has to find the properties to acquire, negotiate the acquisition price, arrange and negotiate financing, and coordinate the due diligence and closing efforts. By now, you should begin to understand how important the asset manager's role is in real estate investment management.

FUNCTION AND GOAL OF PORTFOLIO MANAGEMENT

The portfolio manager has the 10,000-foot view of the assets and primarily communicates with the investor(s). The portfolio manager starts this dialogue by setting investment criteria for the portfolio, such as targeted annual and portfolio reversionary returns. This is a delicate discussion because the portfolio manager wants equity investment from the investors. The investors typically ask for high returns on their equity investments, and the portfolio manager has to decide whether those returns can be achieved, given the portfolio's investment strategy and the current and anticipated market conditions. The portfolio manager's investment strategy defines the type of property invested in and the properties' geographic location, along with maximum concentrations for the various permutations of property type and geographic location. The portfolio manager will manipulate the investment strategy a number of times in an attempt to achieve the returns requested by the investor(s), or convince the investors that perhaps their return criteria may be unachievable, while still being realistic, given market conditions. The worst thing a portfolio manager can agree to is a high rate of return that cannot be achieved. Doing so irreparably affects the portfolio manager's reputation and the portfolio manager may find it difficult to raise equity monies for future transactions.

> *"The more you make something idiot proof, someone is always inventing a better idiot."*
>
> —Heard during roundtable discussion
> at PikeNet Forum, April 3, 2003

The portfolio manager also oversees the asset managers and is responsible for audited financial reporting of the portfolio to the investor(s). The portfolio manager's goal, just like the goal of the property manager and the asset manager, is to increase the value of the property investments to the property's true financial potential.

If done correctly by the portfolio manager and the asset manager, properties can be structured in a way that offsets most down cycles in the market. The structuring on a portfolio management level consists of prudent property type and geographic diversification. The structuring on the asset management level consists of staggering the lease maturities, with associated rental revenue, so that at any given time, occupancy—or more important, debt service coverage—does not drop below a minimum level.

Although these portfolio and asset management strategies are neither easy nor foolproof, they insulate a property and a portfolio from most down cycles in the market.

PROPERTY LIFE CYCLE

At this point in the chapter, I would like to introduce the property life cycle. This property life cycle addresses one specific property.

A property moves through three stages in its life cycle affecting its value: development, stabilization, and then decline. During the stabilization stage, by definition, a property achieves its highest value. If you look closely at Figure 14.3, you will notice that the property's income or value continues to increase during the stabilization stage. Why is this? There are four reasons for this continuing increase in income or value: First, contractual rent increases because of stated escalations in leases; second, rent increases as space is re-leased, presumably at higher market rates; third, use of operating leverage (that is, reduction of operation expenses through efficiencies or more cost-effective services); and fourth, general market conditions.

> *"The commercial real estate market presents an interesting paradox of generally poor property fundamentals and exuberant investor interest."*
>
> —*AEW Research Market Outlook*, Winter-Spring 2004, released February 12, 2004

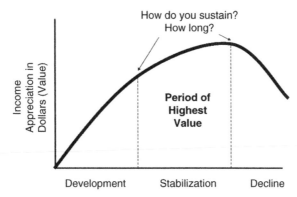

FIGURE 14.3   Real Estate Project Life Cycle

The important question is how long is the stabilization period (depicted by the vertical dashed lines)? The answer is that it lasts as long as you want it to. Understanding the four reasons for continuing value growth during the stabilization stage should show you that as long as you actively manage your property, monitor the market, and make necessary additional (capital) investment, you, in theory, can keep the property in the stabilization stage almost indefinitely. I am really describing the application of the enterprise concept, and it is in the stabilization stage where the application of the enterprise concept is particularly essential if you want to maintain your only goal in real estate development and investment—increase property value. Maintaining and increasing a property's value is essentially up to you and the efforts of the property, asset, and portfolio managers.

If you allow a property to enter the decline stage, you can bring the property back to the stabilization stage, but it is much more difficult. Bringing a property out of decline often requires extensive capital improvements, more so than if you maintained the property in stabilization all along.

LEARNING POINTS FROM THIS CHAPTER

After reading this chapter, I should:

- Understand the relationships between a property manager, an asset manager, and a portfolio manager.
- Know the common goal of the property, asset, and portfolio managers.
- Understand the relationship between the property life cycle and the enterprise concept.

CHAPTER 15

The Future

What's on the horizon for the real estate development industry? As we begin, let's complete (for the moment) our history lesson started at the beginning of the book.

RECENT HISTORY—WHERE WE LEFT OFF

I interrupted the outline of history earlier in this book at about the 1980s. We pick up from the late 1980s into the early 1990s. Up to this point, real estate development and investment in the United States was strong, with an unusually long period of growth and stability. Not many regulations were in place, and investors took advantage of the liberal tax laws and incentives. At this time, banks were not required to obtain appraisals for properties they lent money on. In fact, many real estate projects were done not because they made economic sense but because of the huge tax benefits thrown off by real estate investments and the relatively easy underwriting requirements from banks. There were no limitations, for example, on how much tax losses an investor could deduct on tax returns; the tax benefits could be many multiples for a minimal equity investment. In fact, a building that did not make economic sense maybe reaching only 70 percent occupancy was fantastic for investors because the operating losses as a result of low occupancy meant that investors could deduct even more from their taxable income. Many markets throughout the United States became overbuilt as a result.

Needless to say, this unbridled growth was unsustainable. Many projects defaulted on their bank loans for no other reason than that the cash flow the building generated was insufficient to service the debt. So many projects defaulted that regional economic recessions occurred, particularly in the Southwest United States, and banks who made the loans failed as a result taking back REO (real estate owned). There were so many banks that failed because of the economic environment that the federal government had to step in and form the Resolution Trust Corporation (RTC), a quasi-governmental entity whose sole purpose was to liquidate into the market more than US$300 billion of the REO of the failed banks. While US$300 billion does not seem that much in today's terms, in the late 1980s it was an enormous amount of assets. The RTC liquidated the REO at discounts of upwards of 40 percent, causing a market for investor speculators. During this liquidation period in the early 1990s, essentially no new development occurred; there were exceptions, but those properties were substantially funded by equity and were preleased. This period was one of the most difficult real estate down cycles experienced in the United States. (Interesting—while the details are different, do these characteristics seem similar to the subprime crisis and following credit crisis in the United States in 2008?)

Then came the Tax Reform Act of 1986, which eliminated many of the tax advantages for investing in real estate. For example, it eliminated using accelerated depreciation for tax purposes (properties must now use straight-line depreciation), reinstated the capital gains tax, and created two classes of investors: active and passive investors. Active investors have active involvement in the day-to-day affairs of a real estate project. They are entitled to take the maximum amount of tax deductions due to them. Passive investors are limited to the amount of capital invested in the amount of tax deductions they can take from a real estate project; in essence, they are limited partners. So imagine before the Tax Reform Act of 1986, limited partnerships could not lose (on a cash basis) more than their investment but could deduct unlimited tax benefits. As a result of the Tax Reform Act of 1986, the capital available for real estate essentially disappeared. The federal government also enacted FIRREA (Financial Institutions Reform Recovery and Enforcement Act). Among other things, FIRREA empowered federal mortgage regulators to adopt standards for real estate appraisal and disseminate licensing requirements to the states. Banks, in turn, were now required to obtain appraisals for any real estate loans.

The real estate market and investment methods went through a complete overhaul. This time while the RTC liquidated assets was positive because the market was able to assimilate the assets and create a new paradigm and plan for the future. As the RTC finished liquidating the bank assets, the markets stabilized, and property values increased quickly. There were regulation and transparency in the market, creating an atmosphere of homogeneity and causing the emergence of new and more financial capital sources, particularly from institutional investors such as pension funds. Real estate became institutionalized (no pun intended). Developers realized that large or mega deals were more attractive because large deals took the same amount of effort as a small deal; why not focus on projects that had a bigger impact and more notoriety? (Prior to the 1990s, most projects were relatively small.) In turn, the idea of a true mixed-use project was created. The logic was that each property type has its own up and down cycles. Why not combine different property types that have opposing cycles, thus offsetting the different property type cycles in one mixed-use project? Prior to the 1990s, many developers followed the development philosophy of build it, lease it, sell it. (Consider the three-panel versus four-panel development process chart.) Not much thought was given to the long-term hold of a real estate asset; some did, but this practice was not prevalent in the industry. As a result of the RTC days when there was essentially no trading in the market, developers had to hold onto their properties much longer than they anticipated and realized that in their planning they did not structure their projects with consistent annual project cash flows. Many developers' projects failed or defaulted on their loans because of this lack of consistent annual cash flow. Now, it is required by investors that any commercial real estate project must have consistent annual cash flow; otherwise, it is not considered a prudent investment.

Reflect on what was discussed in this chapter so far: The requirement of appraisals to obtain a bank loan, the requirement for a project to generate consistent annual cash flows, the existence of large projects, and the existence of mixed-use projects are just a few of the phenomena, commonplace today, that started only in the last 15 years or so.

APPARENT FUTURE TRENDS

As I have mentioned several times throughout this book, identifying trends is an essential task of any real estate developer. You learn first about these trends by studying the past. I offered a broad overview in this book, but it is important to read as many real estate development and investment case studies as possible and to speak (network) with as many peers and industry practitioners as possible. I think you understand by now that no two development projects are the same. Hence it is important to learn about the experiences of others and how they resolved their problems and to keep this information in the back of your mind. Parts of any project you do pursue will have similarities to other projects, and it is extremely helpful to be able to refer to similar situations of the past and how they were resolved. I strongly suggest you join several real estate industry professional organizations and attend as many networking events as time and money allow. Not only will you learn about others' problems and solutions but also you are likely to forge relationships that lead to future business opportunities.

Reading case studies and networking will also help you identify future trends (universal knowledge again). Think about what might occur. Do not rely on just the obvious trends, but look for the possible trend beyond the trend. Be observant.

Key development issues today that illustrate current trends are smart growth and place-making. Both topics are a result of the sprawl that has developed throughout the United States. Smart growth is a general phrase directing people to think about how growth occurs and about using what is already in place. Place-making is the concept of programming and designing a project that attracts people to it, thus making a place. Typically, place-making design elements include open, green space with walking paths, benches, or fountains. All cities and residents want developers to address environmental concerns, open space, and traffic congestion. You should address and provide solutions for all of these development issues on any project you wish to put forward; otherwise, you risk having the government and community—not to mention your other constituencies—objecting to your plans.

GREEN DEVELOPMENT AND SMART GROWTH

Green or sustainable development is a clear trend in today's world. Sustainable development integrates economic, environmental, and social considerations into projects of any size. Three elements characterize sustainable development: environmental responsiveness, resource efficiencies, and community and cultural sensitivities. The U.S. Department of Energy has formalized a definition for sustainable design incorporating these three elements. Without going into tremendous detail, the operating premise for sustainable design is to use common sense (turn off lights in unused rooms), do not decimate the existing landscaping (only remove brush and trees necessary to build your building), use natural resources (hydropower of a nearby river to power a project), use recycled products and generate recyclable waste, and design to reflect the local community's predominant culture.

> *"Property has its duties as well as its rights."*
> —Thomas Brummond

Many of the barriers to sustainable development in the United States such as cost premiums are rapidly being eliminated as cities and communities recognize the benefits of sustainable design in buildings. In other areas, such as Western Europe, sustainable development has been occurring for so many years that sustainable development is done as a matter of course. Some of the benefits include:

- Reduction in capital costs: There is a general perception that green building design delays project schedules and raises costs; however, it is starting to be proven that sustainable building design has little effect on project schedules if planned from the beginning and can actually reduce capital costs.
- Reduction in operating costs: Data has begun to show that green buildings generally use 50 to 75 percent less energy than conventionally constructed buildings, so as operating expenses decrease, project value should increase accordingly, because energy savings ultimately improve net operating income.
- Marketing advantages: Project leasing and sale efforts can be significantly improved by utilizing the publicity of new green building projects, and prospective tenants and buyers are attracted to buildings featuring sustainable design elements.

> *"The smallest patch of green to arrest the monotony of asphalt and concrete is as important to the value of real estate as streets, sewers, and convenient shopping."*
> —James Felt, Chairman, New York City Planning Commission,
> *New York Times*, June 28, 1960

- Faster approvals: Generating early and favorable community support for sustainable design projects can significantly speed up approvals (with streamlined approvals becoming a driving strategy for the developer).
- Reduced risk and increased productivity: The U.S. Environmental Protection Agency has ranked indoor air pollution as one of the five top environmental threats to human health. In fact, juries have awarded substantial awards to litigants in indoor air pollution cases involving both private and public facilities.
- Staying ahead of regulations: Many cities are now requiring that buildings meet sustainable design minimums. It is generally more expensive to retroactively comply with new environmental regulations than to design structures that largely anticipate them. Thus, it may be prudent for developers to consider sustainable design building as a viable tool to insulate investments from future regulatory and legal costs.

I think you are probably convinced that sustainable design is a trend that will continue for some time. Again in Europe, sustainable design does not stand out as it does in the United States. Sustainable design techniques are and have been incorporated into projects as a matter of course for hundreds of years. In reality, sustainable design techniques are not new; they have been utilized for literally thousands of years.

What caused the need for smart growth? In short, unbalanced development. This unbalanced development caused the city population to move to new town centers (a continuation of the suburban movement). As suburbs were built, failures in design occurred because of overemphasis on:

- Greenfield development.
- Single-family housing.
- Automobile transportation.
- Isolated land uses.

These failures were considered the hallmarks of suburbanization. It is only recently that we as an industry have found these design characteristics to be misguided and contributing to sprawl. Sprawl weakens the downtown cores that attract and retain young workers and employers—and residents—and reduces choices for different types of communities, resulting in suburbanization or bedroom suburbs. In addition, sprawl through suburbanization caused tremendous decentralization of the cities and imposed redundant costs on communities and taxpayers (states and localities). This decentralization increased demand for new schools, new roads, new public facilities, sewer and water extensions, and more, as well as increasing the redundancy of key services such as police, fire, and emergency medical services. Decentralization through suburbanization relies heavily on property taxes to survive. So logically, if decentralization and suburbanization are reduced (that is, reestablishing our major cities), property taxes should be reduced.

It has also been experienced that cities and metropolitan areas with highly skilled workers (those not having made an exodus to suburban areas) result in cities with higher population, income growth, and tax base, and the cities provide high density and learning environments that excel in creativity and innovation. These cities and metropolitan areas that have high proportions of skilled, educated workers are able to reinvent themselves in down cycles, adapt to changing economic needs, and are attractive to employers, workers, and residents. Hence, developers are being welcomed back into cities and metropolitan areas through incentives and other subsidies.

In summary, some principles and strategies for smart growth include:

- Foster distinctive, attractive communities with a strong sense of place.
- Make development decisions predictable, fair, and cost-effective in the entitlement process, and encourage community and stakeholder collaboration in development decisions.
- Preserve open space, farmland, natural beauty, and critical environmental areas.

A phrase I heard many years ago that I think truly characterizes the principles of smart growth is:

"Create communities, rather than dormitories."

I have come to conclude that real estate development and investment is one of the only professions where you can use the principles of capitalism to make money, yet have a positive social effect on the world creating a place where people live, work, and play.

SOCIAL RESPONSIBILITY AND ETHICS

I devoted an entire chapter at the beginning of this book to business ethics. I want to finish this book by revisiting the topic. Your challenges in today's world are many but often involve your public image. Many communities are still against real estate developers, characterize them as money-hungry, and say that communities, governments, and developers have different agendas.

Know that you are starting your project in a negative position. So it is up to you to educate the community and government and show them that all of the parties have the same objectives; in short, you want to improve the place where people live, work, and play, while everyone makes or saves money. Once your constituencies understand that all of you have the same social and fiscal agenda, the development process will be that much easier. The key to doing this is again education. Through this education—and transparency—you will gain the necessary community support to complete a successful real estate project. Never forget the close-knit nature of the real estate industry. Your personal integrity is everything you have, and you should protect it as much as possible.

> *"Property left to a child may soon be lost; but the inheritance of virtue—a good name and unblemished reputation—will abide forever."*
>
> —William Graham Sumner (1840–1910)

Good luck in your efforts and I wish you success in your real estate development efforts wherever in the world you intend to do a project.

LEARNING POINTS FROM THIS CHAPTER

After reading this chapter, I should:

- Understand what happened in the last major real estate recession in the United States.
- Know the importance of trends and of identifying the trend beyond the trend.
- Appreciate the characteristics of and the need for sustainable design projects.
- Revisit the importance of personal integrity and ethics.

Glossary

abatement (also free rent) Forgiveness of rent payments for a set time, or early occupancy; may occur outside or in addition to the primary term of the lease.

above building standard Upgraded finishes and specialized designs necessary to accommodate a tenant's requirements.

absorption rate The rate at which rentable space is filled. *Gross absorption* is a measure of the total square feet leased over a specified period with no consideration given to space vacated in the same geographic area during the same time period. *Net absorption* is the amount occupied at the end of a period minus the amount occupied at the beginning of a period; it takes into consideration space vacated during the period.

accelerated depreciation A method of cost write-off in which depreciation allowances are greater in the first few years of ownership than in subsequent years. This permits an earlier recovery of capital and a faster tax write-off of an asset.

acre A measure of land equaling 160 square rods, 4,840 square yards, or 43,560 square feet, or a tract about 208.71 feet square.

advance commitment (also take-out commitment or take-out loan commitment) The institutional investor's prior agreement to provide long-term financing upon completion of construction.

air rights The rights in real property to the reasonable use of the air space above the surface of the land.

amenities Satisfaction of enjoyable living to be derived from a home; conditions of agreeable living or a beneficial influence from the location of improvements, not measured in monetary considerations but rather as tangible and intangible benefits attributable to the property, often causing greater pride in ownership.

amortization The liquidation of a financial debt through regular periodic installment payments. For tax purposes, the periodic deduction of capitalized expenses such as organization costs.

amortized loan A loan to be repaid, interest and principal, by a series of regular payments that are equal or nearly equal, without any special balloon payment prior to maturity.

anchor The tenant that serves as the predominant draw to a commercial property, usually the largest tenant in a shopping center.

appraisal An estimate of a property's fair market value that is typically based on replacement cost, discounted cash flow analysis, and/or comparable sales price.

appraiser   One qualified by education, training, and experience who is hired to estimate the value of real and personal property based on experience, judgment, facts, and use of formal appraisal processes.

appreciation   An increase in the value or price of an asset.

assessment   A fee imposed on property, usually to pay for public improvements such as water, sewers, streets, and improvement districts.

asset management   The various disciplines involved with managing real property assets from the time of investment through the time of disposition, including acquisition, management, leasing, operational/financial reporting, appraisals, audits, market review, and asset disposition plans.

asset management fee   A fee charged to investors based on the amount invested into real estate assets for the fund or account.

assignment   A transfer of the lessee's entire stake in the property. It is distinguishable from a sublease, where the sublessee acquires something less than the lessee's entire interest.

assignment of rent   A provision in a deed of trust (or mortgage) under which the beneficiary may, upon default by the trustor, take possession of the property, collect income from the property, and apply it to the loan balance and the costs incurred by the beneficiary.

attorn   To agree to recognize a new owner of a property and to pay him or her rent.

average free rent   Expressed in months, the rent abatement concession expected to be granted to a tenant as part of a lease incentive under current market conditions.

average occupancy   The average occupancy rate of each of the preceding 12 months.

average total assets   Calculated by adding the total assets of a company for the five most recent quarters and dividing by five.

balloon (or bullet) loan   A loan with a maturity that is shorter than the amortization period.

bankrupt   The state of an entity that is unable to repay its debts as they become due.

bankruptcy   Proceedings under federal statutes to relieve a debtor who is unable or unwilling to pay debts. After addressing certain priorities and exemptions, the bankrupt entity's property and other assets are distributed by the court to creditors as full satisfaction for the debt.

base rent   A set amount used as a minimum rent, with provisions for increasing the rent over the term of the lease.

base year   Actual taxes and operating expenses for a specified year, most often the year in which a lease commences.

bearing wall   A wall or partition that supports a part of a building, usually a roof or floor above.

below-grade   Any structure or portion of a structure located underground or below the surface grade of the surrounding land.

blighted area   A district affected by detrimental influences of such extent or quantity that real property values have seriously declined as a result of adverse land use and/or destructive economic forces; characterized by rapidly depreciating buildings, retrogression, and no recognizable prospects for improvement. However, renewal programs and changes in use may lead to resurgence of such areas.

blockbusting The practice on the part of unscrupulous speculators or real estate agents of inducing panic selling of homes at prices below market value, especially by exploiting the prejudices of property owners in neighborhoods in which the racial makeup is changing or appears to be on the verge of changing.

book value Also referred to as common shareholder's equity, this is the total shareholder's equity as of the most recent quarterly balance sheet, minus preferred stock and redeemable preferred stock.

breakeven analysis A cash flow technique that shows for predetermined times the net income or net expenditures of a project and its break-even point. Often a breakeven analysis includes debt service payments.

broker A person who acts as an intermediary between two or more parties in connection with a transaction.

brown-field site A site which has previously been developed and is available for redevelopment. Sometimes such a site has the remains of former buildings and may have environmental contamination.

buildable acres The area of land that is available to be built on after subtracting for roads, setbacks, anticipated open spaces, and areas unsuitable for construction.

building code The various laws set forth by the governing municipality as to the end use of a certain piece of property. They dictate the criteria for design, materials, and types of improvements allowed.

building line A line set by law a certain distance from a street line, in front of which an owner cannot build on the owner's lot. A setback line.

building permit Written government permission to develop, renovate, or repair a building.

building standard plus allowance The landlord lists, in detail, the building standard materials and costs necessary to make the premises suitable for occupancy. A negotiated allowance is then provided for the tenant to customize or upgrade materials.

build-out Space improvements put in place per the tenant's specifications. Takes into consideration the amount of tenant finish allowance provided in the lease agreement, including flooring, walls, finished plumbing, and electrical work.

build-to-suit A method of leasing property whereby the developer or landlord builds to a tenant's specifications.

bundle of rights All of the legal rights incident to ownership of property, including rights of use, possession, encumbering, and disposition.

capital expenditures Investment of cash or the creation of a liability to acquire or improve an asset, as distinguished from cash outflows for expense items that are considered part of normal operations.

capital improvements Expenditures that arrest deterioration of property or add new improvements and appreciably prolong its life.

capital markets Public and private markets where businesses or individuals can raise or borrow capital.

capitalization rate The rate at which net operating income is discounted to determine the value of a property. It is the net operating income divided by the sales price or value of a property expressed as a percentage.

carrying or carry charges Costs incidental to property ownership that must be absorbed by the landlord during the initial lease-up of a building and thereafter during periods of vacancy.

cash flow The revenue remaining after all cash expenses are paid.

cash-on-cash yield The relationship, expressed as a percentage, between the net cash flow of a property and the average amount of invested capital during an operating year.

certificate of occupancy A document presented by a local government agency or building department certifying that a building and/or the leased area has been satisfactorily inspected and is in a condition suitable for occupancy.

chain of title A history of conveyances and encumbrances affecting the title from the time the original patent was granted, or as far back as records are available, used to determine how title came to be vested in the current owner.

Class A A real estate rating generally assigned to properties that will generate the highest rents per square foot because of their high quality and/or superior location.

Class B Good assets that most tenants would find desirable but that lack attributes that would permit owners to charge the highest rents.

Class C Buildings that offer few amenities but are otherwise in physically acceptable condition and provide cost-effective space to tenants who are not particularly image-conscious.

clear-span facility A building, most often a warehouse or parking garage, with vertical columns on the outside edges of the structure and a clear span between columns.

commercial property Other than residential. Owned or leased property such as office, research, retail, and industrial properties. Multi-family residential apartments are considered commercial property.

commitment A pledge, promise, or firm agreement to do something in the future, such as a loan company giving a written commitment with the specific terms of a mortgage loan it will make.

common area For lease purposes, the areas of a building and its site that are available for the nonexclusive use of all its tenants, such as lobbies and corridors.

common area maintenance Rent charged to the tenant in addition to the base rent to maintain the common areas. Examples include snow removal, outdoor lighting, parking lot sweeping, insurance, and property taxes.

common law The body of law that grew from customs and practices developed and used in England.

comparables Properties with similar characteristics used to determine the fair market lease rate or asking price of a property.

concessions Cash or cash equivalents expended by the landlord in the form of rental abatement, additional tenant finish allowance, moving expenses, or other monies expended to influence or persuade a tenant to sign a lease.

condemnation The process of taking private property, without the consent of the owner, by a governmental agency for public use through the power of eminent domain.

condominium An estate in real property wherein there is an undivided interest in common in a portion of real property coupled with a separate interest in space called a unit, the boundaries of which are described on a recorded final map, parcel map, or condominium plan. The areas within the boundaries may be filled with air, earth, water, or any combination and need not be attached to land except by easements for access and support.

condominium declaration The document that establishes a condominium and describes the property rights of the unit owners.

consideration Anything given or promised by a party to induce another to enter into a contract, such as personal services or even love and affection. It may be a benefit conferred upon one party or a detriment suffered by the other.

constant or loan constant The percentage that, when applied directly to the face value of a debt, develops the annual amount of money necessary to pay a specified net rate of interest on the reducing balance and to liquidate the debt in a specified time period. For example, a 6 percent loan with a 20-year amortization has a constant of approximately 8.5 percent. Thus, a US$10,000 loan amortized over 20 years requires an annual payment of approximately US$850.

construction loan A loan made to finance the actual construction or improvement on land. Funds are usually dispersed in increments as the construction progresses. Interim financing during the developmental phase of a property.

construction management The act of ensuring that the various stages of the construction process are completed in a timely and seamless fashion. Construction supervision by a qualified manager.

Consumer Price Index (CPI) Measures inflation in relation to the change in the price of goods and services purchased by a specified population during a base period of time. The CPI is commonly used to increase the base rent periodically as a means of protecting the landlord's rental stream against inflation or to provide a cushion for operating expense increases for a landlord unwilling to undertake the record keeping necessary for operating expense escalations.

contiguous space Multiple suites or spaces within the same building and on the same floor that can be combined and rented to a single tenant, or a block of space located on multiple adjoining floors in a building.

contract A legal agreement between entities that requires each to conduct (or refrain from conducting) certain activities. This document provides each party with a right that is enforceable under a judicial system.

contract documents The complete set of design plans and specifications for the construction of a building.

contract rent (also face rent) The rental obligation, expressed in dollars, as specified in a lease.

convertible debt A mortgage position that gives the lender the option to convert to a partial or full ownership position in a property within a specified time period.

convertible preferred stock Preferred stock that is convertible to common stock under certain formulas and conditions specified by the issuer of the stock.

conveyance Most commonly refers to the transfer of title to property between parties by deed. The term may also include most of the instruments with which an interest in real estate is created, mortgaged, or assigned.

core properties The major property types, specifically office, retail, industrial, and multifamily. Core assets tend to be built within the past five years or recently renovated. They are substantially leased (90 percent or better) with higher-credit tenants and well-structured long-term leases, with the majority fairly early in the term of the lease. Core assets generate good, stable income that, together with potential appreciation, is expected to generate total returns in the 10 percent to 12 percent range.

covenant A written agreement inserted into deeds or other legal instruments stipulating performance or nonperformance of certain acts, or use or nonuse of a property and/or land (e.g., no bars that serve alcohol).

credit enhancement The credit support needed in addition to the mortgage collateral to achieve a desired credit rating on mortgage-backed securities. The forms of credit enhancement most often employed are subordination, overcollateralization, reserve funds, corporate guarantees, and letters of credit.

current occupancy The current leased portion of a building or property expressed as a percentage of its total area or units.

deal structure With regard to the financing of an acquisition, deals can be unleveraged, leveraged, traditional debt, participating debt, participating/convertible debt, or joint ventures.

debt service The outlay necessary to meet all interest and principal payments during a given period.

debt service coverage ratio (DSCR) The annual net operating income from a property divided by annual cost of debt service. A DSCR below 1 means the property is generating insufficient cash flow to cover debt payments.

dedicate To appropriate private property to public ownership for a public use.

deed A legal instrument transferring title to real property from the seller to the buyer upon the sale of such property.

deed in lieu of foreclosure A deed to real property accepted by a lender from a defaulting borrower to avoid the necessity of foreclosure proceedings by the lender.

deed restriction An imposed restriction in a deed that limits the use of the property. For example, a restriction could prohibit the sale of alcoholic beverages.

default The general failure to perform a legal or contractual duty or to discharge an obligation when due.

defeasance clause The clause in a mortgage that gives the mortgagor the right to redeem mortgagor's property upon the payment of mortgagor's obligations to the mortgagee.

demising wall The partition wall that separates one tenant's space from another's or from the building's common areas.

depreciation A decrease or loss in property value due to wear, age, or other cause. In accounting, depreciation is a periodic allowance made for this real or implied loss.

design/build   A system in which a single entity is responsible for both the design and construction.

developer's fee   Usually stated as a percentage of development cost or as a fixed dollar amount.

discount rate   A yield rate used to convert future payments or receipts into present value.

discounted cash flow analysis (DCF)   Techniques used in investment and development appraisal whereby future inflows and outflows of cash associated with a particular project are expressed in present-day terms by discounting. The most widely used forms of DCF are the internal rate of return (IRR) and the net present value (NPV). The techniques may be used for such purposes as the valuation of land and investments, the ranking of projects and evaluating the design of projects or their components.

diversification   The process of consummating individual investments in a manner that insulates a portfolio against the risk of reduced yield or capital loss, accomplished by allocating individual investments among a variety of asset types, each with different characteristics.

dollar stop   An agreed dollar amount of taxes and operating expense each tenant will pay on a prorated basis.

draw   Usually applies to construction loans when disbursement of a portion of the mortgage is advanced as improvements to the property are made.

due diligence   Activities carried out by a prospective purchaser or mortgagor of real property to confirm that the property is as represented by the seller and is not subject to environmental or other problems. In the case of an IPO registration statement, due diligence is a reasonable investigation by the parties involved to confirm that all the statements within the document are true and that no material facts are omitted.

earnest money (or deposit)   The monetary advance of part of the purchase price to indicate the intention and ability of the buyer to carry out the contract.

easement   A right created by grant, reservation, agreement, prescription, or necessary implication to use someone else's property.

effective gross income (EGI)   The total income from a property generated by rents and other sources, less a vacancy factor estimated to be appropriate for the property. EGI is expressed as collected income before expenses and debt service.

effective gross rent (EGR)   The net rent generated, after adjusting for tenant improvements and other capital costs, lease commissions, and other sales expenses.

effective rent   The actual rental rate to be achieved by the landlord after deducting the value of concessions from the base rental rate paid by a tenant, usually expressed as an average rate over the term of the lease.

eminent domain   A power to acquire by condemnation private property for public use in return for just compensation.

encroachment   The intrusion of a structure that extends, without permission, over a property line, easement boundary, or building setback line

encumbrance   A right to, or interest in, real property held by someone other than the owner that does not prevent the transfer of fee title.

environmental impact statement Documents required by federal and state laws to accompany proposals for major projects and programs that are likely to have an impact on the surrounding environment.

equity The residual value of a property beyond mortgage or liability. The amount contributed in cash or property.

escalation The mechanism in a lease that increases the rent, usually annually. May be set forth in fixed steps, tied to increases in operating expenses, or tied to increases in the Consumer Price Index (CPI).

escalation clause A clause in a lease that provides for the rent to be increased to reflect changes in expenses paid by the landlord, such as real estate taxes and operating costs.

escrow agreement A written agreement made between an escrow agent and the parties to a contract setting forth the basic obligations of the parties, describing the money (or other things of value) to be deposited in escrow, and instructing the escrow agent concerning the disposition of the monies deposited.

estoppel certificate A signed statement certifying that certain statements of fact are correct as of the date of the statement and can be relied upon by a third party, including a prospective lender or purchaser.

ethics That branch of moral science, idealism, justness, and fairness, that treats the duties a member of a profession or craft owes to the public, client or partner, and to professional brethren or members. Accepted standards of right and wrong. Moral conduct, behavior, or duty.

exclusive agency listing A written agreement between a real estate broker and a property owner in which the owner promises to pay a fee or commission to the broker if specified real property is leased during the listing period.

exit strategy Strategy available to investors when they desire to liquidate all or part of their investment, which should be detailed throughout a project's or investment's life.

façade The front of a building; often used to refer to a false front.

face rental rate The asking rental rate published by the landlord.

facility space The floor area in hospitality properties dedicated to operating departments, such as restaurants, health clubs, and gift shops, that service multiple guests or the general public on an interactive basis not directly related to room occupancy.

fair market value The sale price at which a property would change hands between a willing buyer and willing seller, neither being under any compulsion to buy or sell and both having reasonable knowledge of the relevant facts.

Fannie Mae (FNMA) The Federal National Mortgage Association, a quasi-governmental corporation authorized to sell debentures in order to supplement private mortgage funds by buying and selling FHA (Federal Housing Administration) and VA (Veterans Affairs) loans at market prices.

Federal Housing Administration (FHA) An agency of the federal government that insures private mortgage loans for financing new and existing homes and home repairs.

fee simple interest When an owner owns all the rights in a real estate parcel.

fiduciary A person who represents another on financial and/or property matters. That duty owed by an agent to act in the highest good faith toward the principal and not to obtain any advantage over the latter by the slightest misrepresentation, concealment, duress, or pressure.

first mortgage The senior mortgage that, by reason of its position, has priority over all junior encumbrances. The holder has a priority right to payment in the event of default.

first refusal right (or right of first refusal) A lease clause giving a tenant the first opportunity to buy a property or lease additional space in a property at the same price and on the same terms and conditions as those contained in a third-party offer that the owner has expressed a willingness to accept.

fixed costs Costs that do not fluctuate in proportion to the level of sales or production.

fixed rate An interest rate that remains constant over the term of the loan.

fixtures Personal property so attached the land or building (e.g., improvements) that it is considered part of the real property.

flex space A building that provides a configuration allowing occupants a flexible amount of office or showroom space in combination with manufacturing, laboratory, warehouse, or distribution.

floor area ratio (FAR) The ratio of the gross square footage of a building to the square footage of the land on which it is situated.

force majeure A force that cannot be controlled by the parties to a contract and prevents them from complying with the provisions of the contract. This includes acts of God, such as a flood or a hurricane, and acts of man, such as a strike, fire, or war.

foreclosure The process by which the trustee or servicer takes over a property from a borrower on behalf of the lender.

forward commitments Contractual obligations to perform certain financing activities upon the satisfaction of any stated conditions. Usually used to describe a lender's obligation to fund a mortgage.

Freddie Mac (FHLMC) Federal Home Loan Mortgage Corp., a corporation established by the Federal Home Loan Bank to issue mortgage-backed securities.

full recourse (or recourse) A loan on which an endorser or guarantor is liable in the event of default by the borrower.

full-service rent An all-inclusive rental rate that includes operating expenses and real estate taxes for the first year. The tenant is generally still responsible for any increase in operating expenses over the base year amount.

future proposed space Space in a proposed commercial development that is not yet under construction or where no construction start date has been set. It also may refer to the future phases of a multiphase project not yet built.

general contractor The prime contractor who contracts for the construction of an entire building or project, rather than just a portion of the work. The general contractor hires subcontractors, coordinates all work, and is responsible for payment to subcontractors.

general partner A member of a partnership who has authority to bind the partnership and shares in the profits and losses of the partnership.

go-dark   The condition that results from a tenant's closing its business, even though the lease is still in effect; typically applicable to retail businesses. Lease language may provide a means for a landlord to void a lease and take back the leased premises if the tenant ceases to operate its business at that location.

going-in capitalization rate   The capitalization rate computed by dividing the projected first year's net operating income by the value of the property.

graduated lease   A lease, generally long-term in nature, in which rent varies depending upon future contingencies.

greenfield site   Land that is or is potentially available for development but that has not been developed before (e.g., agricultural land).

gross building area   The sum of areas at each floor level, including basements, mezzanines, and penthouses, within the principal outside faces of the exterior walls and neglecting architectural setbacks or projections.

gross leasable area   The portion of total floor area designed for tenants' occupancy and exclusive use, including storage areas. It is the total area that produces rental income.

gross lease   A lease in which the tenant pays a flat sum for rent, out of which the landlord must pay all expenses, such as taxes, insurance, maintenance, and utilities.

gross square feet   Usually refers to gross area of a building by measuring from the outside of its exterior walls and including all vertical penetrations, such as elevator shafts. Also includes basement space.

ground lease (or land lease)   A long-term lease of land, entered into by a tenant to construct a building (at its expense) from which to conduct its business.

ground rent   Rent paid to the owner for use of land, normally on which to build a building. Generally, the arrangement is that of a long-term lease (e.g., 99 years) with the lessor retaining title to the land.

guarantor   One who makes a guaranty.

guaranty   Agreement whereby the guarantor assures satisfaction of the debt of another or performs the obligation of another if and when the debtor fails to do so.

hard cost   The cost of actually constructing property improvements.

highest and best use   The reasonably probable and legal use of vacant land or an improved property that is physically possible, appropriately supported, and financially feasible and that results in the highest value.

holdbacks   A portion of a loan commitment that is not funded until an additional requirement is met, such as completion of construction.

holding period   The length of time an investor expects to own a property from purchase to sale.

holdover tenant   A tenant retaining possession of the leased premises after the expiration of a lease.

HUD   The Department of Housing and Urban Development, which is responsible for the implementation and administration of U.S. government housing and urban development programs.

HVAC   The acronym for heating, ventilating, and air conditioning.

hybrid debt   A mortgage position with equity-like participation features in both cash flow and the appreciation of the property at the time of sale or refinance; often mezzanine financing is considered hybrid debt.

improvements   In the context of leasing, the improvements made to or inside a building; may include any permanent structure or other development, such as a street, sidewalk, or utilities.

income capitalization value   The indication of value derived for an income-producing property by converting its anticipated benefits into property value through direct capitalization of expected income or by discounting the annual cash flows for the holding period at a specified yield rate.

income property   Real estate that is owned or operated to produce revenue.

income return   The percentage of the total return that is generated by the income from operations of a property, fund, or account.

indirect costs   Development costs other than direct material and labor costs that are directly related to the construction of improvements, including administrative and office expenses, commissions, and architectural, engineering, and financing costs.

inflation   The annual rate at which consumer prices increase.

inflation hedge   An investment that tends to increase in value at a rate greater than inflation and contributes to the preservation of the purchasing power of a portfolio.

interest   The price paid for the use of capital.

internal rate of return (IRR)   A discounted cash-flow analysis calculation used to determine the potential total return of a real estate asset during an anticipated holding period.

inventory   All space within a certain proscribed market without regard to its availability or condition.

joint tenancy   Ownership of real property by two or more individuals, each of whom has an undivided interest with the right of survivorship.

joint venture   An investment entity formed by one or more entities to acquire or develop and manage real property and/or other assets.

judgment   A formal decision issued by a court relating to the specific claims and rights of the parties to an act or suit.

just compensation   Compensation that is fair to both the owner and the public when property is taken for public use through condemnation (eminent domain).

landlord   One who rents property to a tenant.

lease   An agreement whereby the owner of real property gives the right of possession to another for a specified period of time and for a specified consideration.

lease commencement date   The date that usually constitutes the commencement of the term of the lease, regardless of whether the tenant has actually taken possession, so long as beneficial occupancy is possible.

lease expiration exposure schedule (or lease maturity schedule)   A listing of the total square footage of all current leases that expire in each of the next five years, without regard to renewal options.

leasehold improvements   Construction or improvements for the purpose of preparing the premises for the conduct of the tenant's business. Improvements permanently attach to the premises unless they are trade fixtures, and they remain with the premises after the end of term of the lease.

leasehold interest The right to hold or use property for a fixed period of time at a given price, without transfer of ownership.

legal description A geographical description identifying a parcel by government survey, metes and bounds, or lot numbers of a recorded plat, including a description of any portion that is subject to an easement or reservation.

legal owner The legal owner has title to the property, although the title may actually carry no rights to the property other than as a lien.

lessee An individual (i.e., tenant) to whom property is rented under a lease.

lessor An individual (i.e., landlord) who rents property to a tenant via a lease.

letter of credit A commitment by a bank or other person that the issuer will honor drafts or other demands for payment upon full compliance with the conditions specified in the letter of credit. Letters of credit are often used in place of cash deposited with the landlord in satisfying the security deposit provisions of a lease.

letter of intent A preliminary agreement stating the proposed terms for a final contract.

leverage (financial) The use of credit to finance a portion of the costs of purchasing or developing a real estate investment. Positive leverage occurs when the interest rate is lower than the capitalization rate or projected internal rate of return. Negative leverage occurs when the current return on equity is diminished by the employment of debt.

leverage (operating) The adjustment of operating expenses, and sometimes revenues, to improve the net operating income of a project and thus its value.

LIBOR (London Interbank Offered Rate) The interest rate offered on Eurodollar deposits traded between banks, also called swaps.

lien A claim or encumbrance against property used to secure a debt, a charge, or the performance of some act.

lien waiver Waiver of a mechanic's lien rights that is often required before the general contractor can receive a draw under the payment provisions of a construction contract. It may also be required before the owner can receive a draw on a construction loan.

life cycle The various developmental stages of a property predevelopment, development, leasing, operating, and redevelopment (or rehab).

limited partnership A type of partnership comprised of one or more general partners who manage the business and are personally liable for partnership debts, and one or more limited partners who contribute capital and share in profits but who take no part in running the business and incur no liability above the amount contributed.

liquidity The ease with which assets can be converted to cash without loss in value.

lis pendens A notice filed or recorded for the purpose of warning all persons that the title or right to the possession of certain real property is in litigation; literally, suit pending; usually recorded to give constructive notice of pending litigation.

listing agreement   An agreement between the owner of a property and a real estate broker giving the broker authorization to attempt to sell or lease the property at a certain price and terms in return for a commission, set fee, or other form of compensation.

load factor   The amount of square footage in a lease, in addition to a tenant's usable square footage, which represents the tenant's pro rata share of the building's common areas. May also be referred to as a percentage of building's rentable square feet.

loan-to-value ratio (LTV)   The ratio of the value of the loan principal divided by the property's appraised value.

long-term lease   In most markets, a lease whose term is at least three years from initial signing to the date of expiration or renewal.

loss factor   Percentage of the gross area of a space lost to walls, elevator, and the like. The rule of thumb in Manhattan, for example, is approximately 15 percent.

lot   Generally one of several contiguous parcels of land making up a fractional part or subdivision of a block, the boundaries of which are shown on recorded maps and plats.

low-rise   A building with fewer than four stories above ground level.

lump-sum contract   A type of construction contract requiring the general contractor to complete a building or project for a fixed cost normally established by competitive bidding. The contractor absorbs any loss or retains any profit.

market price   The actual selling or leasing price of a property.

market rental rates   The rental income that a property most likely would command in the open market, indicated by the current rents asked and paid for comparable space.

market study   A forecast of future demand for a certain type of real estate project that includes an estimate of the square footage that can be absorbed and the rents that can be charged.

market value   The highest price a property would command in a competitive and open market under all conditions requisite to a fair sale.

marketable title   A title free from encumbrances that could be readily marketed to a willing purchaser.

master lease   A primary lease that controls subsequent leases and may cover more property than subsequent leases.

maturity date   The date when the total principal balance comes due.

mechanic's lien   A claim created for the purpose of securing priority of payment of the price and value of work performed and materials furnished in constructing, repairing, or improving a building or other structure.

meeting of the minds   When all individuals to a contract agree to the substance and terms of that contract.

metes and bounds   The boundary lines of land described by listing the compass directions and distances of the boundaries. Originally, metes referred to distance and bounds referred to direction.

mezzanine financing (see hybrid debt)   Somewhere between equity and debt, that piece of the capital structure that has senior debt above it and equity below it. There is both equity and debt mezzanine financing; it can be done at the asset or company level, or it could be unrated tranches of commercial mortgage-backed securities (CMBS). Returns are generally in the mid- to high teens.

mile   5,280 feet.

mixed-use   Space within a building or project providing for more than one property use.

mortgage   A legal document by which real property is pledged as security for repayment of a loan until the debt is repaid in full.

mortgage constant   The ratio of an amortizing mortgage payment to the outstanding mortgage balance.

NAREIT (National Association of Real Estate Investment Trusts)   The national, not-for-profit trade organization that represents the real estate investment trust industry.

negative amortization   The accrual feature found in numerous participating debt structures that allows an investor to pay, for an initial period of time, an interest rate below the contract rate stated in loan documents.

net cash flow   Generally determined by net income plus depreciation less principal payments on long-term mortgages.

net income   The money remaining after expenses are deducted from income; the profit.

net lease (also single, double, and triple net lease)   The lessee pays not only a fixed rental charge but also expenses on the rented property, including maintenance.

net operating income (NOI)   A before-tax computation of gross revenue less operating expenses and an allowance for anticipated vacancy. It is a key indicator of financial strength.

net present value (NPV)   Usually employed to evaluate the relative merits of two or more investment alternatives, the sum of the total present value of incremental future cash flows plus the present value of estimated proceeds from sale. Whenever the net present value is greater than zero, an investment opportunity is generally considered to have merit.

noncompete clause   A clause that can be inserted into a lease specifying that the business of the tenant is exclusive in the property and that no other tenant operating the same or similar type of business can occupy space in the building. This clause benefits service-oriented businesses desiring exclusive access to the building's population.

nondisturbance agreement   Tenants sign this to prevent themselves from being evicted if the property owner does not pay its mortgage to the bank.

nonperforming loan   A loan that is unable to meet its contractual principal and interest payments.

nonrecourse debt   A loan that, in the event of a default by the borrower, limits the lender's remedies to a foreclosure of the mortgage, realization on its assignment of leases and rents, and acquisition of the real estate.

off-site improvements Work not on the subject project site to make the subject project site suitable for development or improvement, e.g., roads, side walks, water mains, or sewers.

open space An area of land or water dedicated for public or private use or enjoyment.

operating cost escalation Escalation clause intended to adjust rents by reference to external standards, such as published indexes, negotiated wage levels, or expenses related to the ownership and operation of a building.

operating expense The actual costs associated with operating a property, including maintenance, repairs, management, utilities, taxes, and insurance.

option A right given to purchase or lease a property upon specified terms within a specified time. If the right is not exercised, the option holder is not subject to liability for damages. If the holder of the option exercises it, the grantor of the option must perform the option's requirements.

oral contract A verbal agreement not reduced to writing.

orientation Placing a structure on its lot with regard to its exposure to the rays of the sun, prevailing winds, privacy from the street, and protection from outside noises.

out-parcel (also pad) Individual building site in a shopping center exterior of main building(s).

parking ratio Dividing the total rentable square footage of a building by the building's total number of parking spaces provides the amount of rentable square feet per each individual parking space.

partial recourse A loan on which an endorser or guarantor is liable for a limited time in the event of default by the borrower.

partial taking The taking of part of an owner's property under the laws of eminent domain.

participation debt In addition to collecting a contract interest rate, participating debt allows the lender to have participatory equity rights through a share of increases in income and/or increases in residual value over the loan balance or original value at the time of loan funding.

pass-through expense An expense associated with tenancy in which the landlord passes through to a tenant certain increases in building operating expenses occurring after a base year in the lease.

percentage rent Rent payable under a lease that is equal to a percentage of gross sales or gross revenues received by the tenant. It is commonly used in retail center leases. There is usually a clause for a minimum rent as well.

performance bond A surety bond posted by a contractor guaranteeing full performance of a contract, with the proceeds to be used to complete the contract or compensate for the owner's loss in the event of nonperformance.

permanent loan The long-term mortgage on a property.

personal property Any property that is not real property, such as furniture, clothing, and artwork.

Planning Commission An agency of local government charged with planning the development, redevelopment, or preservation of an area.

plat Map of a specific area, such as a subdivision, that shows the boundaries of individual lots, together with streets and easements.

police power The right of the state to enact laws and enforce them for the order, safety, health, morals, and general welfare of the public.

portfolio management Formulating, modifying, and implementing a real estate investment strategy in light of an investor's broader overall investment objectives; management of several properties owned by a single entity.

preleased Space in a proposed building that has been leased before the start of construction or in advance of the issuance of a certificate of occupancy.

premises In commercial real estate, the description of the leasehold and the specific square footage for which the parties enter into a lease.

prepayment penalty The charge payable to a lender by a borrower under the terms of the loan agreement if the borrower pays off the outstanding principal balance of the loan prior to its maturity.

prepayment rights Rights given to the borrower to make partial or full payment of the total principal balance prior to the maturity date without penalty.

prime space First-generation space that is available for lease.

prime tenant The major tenant in a building, or the major or anchor tenant in a shopping center.

principal payments The return of invested capital to the lender, often through amortization.

privity Mutual relationship to the same rights of property; contractual relationship.

privity of contract The relationship between the persons who are parties to a contract.

pro rata In proportion; according to a certain percentage or proportion of a whole. In the case of a tenant, the proportionate share of expenses for the maintenance and operation of the property.

proration Adjustments of interest, taxes, insurance, and the like on a pro rata basis as of the closing or agreed-upon date. Fire insurance is normally paid for three years in advance. If a property is sold during this time, the seller wants a refund on that portion of the advance payment that has not been used at the time the title to the property is transferred. For example, if the property is sold two years later, the seller will want a third of the advance premium that was paid. Usually done in escrow by the escrow holder at time of closing the transaction.

public records Records that by law impart constructive notice of matters relating to land.

punch list An itemized list documenting incomplete or unsatisfactory items after the contractor has notified the owner that the tenant space is substantially complete; upon remedy and completion, usually fulfills the obligations of the contractor under a construction contract.

quiet enjoyment The right of a landlord or tenant to use the property without disturbances.

quitclaim deed A deed operating as a release that is intended to pass any title, interest, or claim that the grantor may have in the property, but not guaranteeing such title is valid.

raw land   Unimproved land that remains in its natural state.

raw space   Unimproved shell space in a building.

real estate syndicate   When partners (either with or without unlimited liability) form a partnership to participate in a real estate venture.

real property   Land, and generally whatever is affixed to the land.

recording   The process of placing a document on file for public notice with a designated public official, usually a county recorder, who designates the fact that a document has been presented for recording by placing a recording stamp upon it indicating the time of day and the date when it was officially placed on file. Documents filed with the recorder are considered to be placed on open notice to the general public of that county. Claims against property usually are given a priority on the basis of the time and the date they are recorded, with the most preferred claim going to the earliest one recorded, the next claim going to the next earliest one recorded, and so on. This type of notice is called constructive notice or legal notice.

recourse   The right of a lender, in the event of default by the borrower, to recover against the personal assets of a party who is secondarily liable for the debt.

refinancing   The paying off of an existing obligation and assuming a new obligation in its place; financing anew, or extending or renewing existing financing.

rehab   Extensive renovation intended to cure obsolescence of a building or project.

REIT (Real Estate Investment Trust)   A business trust or corporation that combines the capital of many investors to acquire or provide financing for real estate. It generally does not pay corporate income tax to the IRS. Instead, it pays out at least 90 percent of its taxable income in the form of dividends.

renewal option   A clause giving a tenant the right to extend the term of a lease.

renewal probability   Used to estimate leasing-related costs and downtime, it is the average percentage of tenants in a building that are expected to renew at market rental rates upon the expiration of their leases.

rent   Compensation or fee paid for the occupancy and use of any rental property, land, buildings, equipment, or the like.

rent commencement date   The date on which a tenant begins paying rent, which may be different from the lease commencement date when certain obligations must be fulfilled, such as the construction of tenant improvements.

rentable/usable ratio   A building's total rentable area divided by its usable area. It represents the tenant's pro-rata share of the building's common areas and can determine the square footage on which the tenant will pay rent. The inverse describes the proportion of space that an occupant can expect to actually use.

rental concession   What landlords offer tenants to secure their tenancy. Rental abatement is one form of concession; others include increased tenant improvement allowance, signage, below-market rental rates, and moving allowances.

rental growth rate   The expected trend in market rental rates over the period of analysis, expressed as an annual percentage increase.

rent-up period   The period following construction of a new building, when tenants are actively sought and the project is approaching its stabilized occupancy.

REO (Real Estate Owned)   Real estate owned by a savings institution as a result of default by borrowers and subsequent foreclosure by the institution.

replacement cost   The estimated current cost to construct a building with utility equivalent to the building being appraised, using modern materials and current standards, design, and layout.

replacement reserves   An allowance that provides for the periodic replacement of building components that wear out more rapidly than the building itself and must be replaced during the building's economic life.

reproduction cost   The cost of replacing the subject improvement with one that is the exact replica, having the same quality of workmanship, design, and layout, or the cost to duplicate an asset.

rescission of contract   The abrogation or annulling of a contract; the revocation or repealing of a contract by mutual consent of the parties to the contract or for cause by either party to the contract.

reserve account   An account that a borrower has to fund to protect the lender. Examples include capital expenditure accounts and deferred maintenance accounts.

Resolution Trust Corporation (RTC)   The RTC was established by Congress in 1989 to contain, manage, and sell failed savings institutions and recover taxpayer funds through the management and sale of the institutions' assets.

retention rate   The percent of trailing 12-month earnings that have been plowed back into the company. It is calculated as 100 minus the trailing 12-month payout ratio.

reversion capitalization rate   The capitalization rate used to determine reversion value.

reversion value   A lump-sum benefit that an investor receives or expects to receive at the termination of an investment.

RevPAR (Revenue per Available Room)   Total room revenue for the period divided by the average number of available rooms in a hospitality facility.

right of survivorship   The right of a surviving tenant or tenants to succeed to the entire interest of the deceased tenant; the distinguishing feature of a joint tenancy.

right of way   A privilege operating as an easement upon land, whereby the owner by grant or by agreement gives another the right to pass over the owner's land, to construct a roadway, or to use as a roadway a specific part of the land; the right to construct through and over the land telephone, telegraph, or electric power lines; or the right to place underground water mains, gas mains, or sewer mains.

risk management   A systematic approach to identifying and separating insurable risks from noninsurable risks and evaluating the availability and costs of purchasing third-party insurance.

roll-over risk   The risk that a tenant's lease will not be renewed.

sale-leaseback   An arrangement by which the owner-occupant of a property agrees to sell all or part of the property to an investor and then lease it back and continue to occupy space as a tenant.

sales comparison value A value indication derived by comparing the property being appraised with similar properties that have been sold recently.

secondary financing A loan on real property secured by a lien junior to an existing first mortgage loan.

secondary market A market where existing mortgage loans are securitized and then bought and sold to other investors.

second-generation or secondary space Previously occupied space that becomes available for lease, either directly from the landlord or as sublease space.

security deposit A deposit of money by a tenant to a landlord to secure performance of a lease. It also can take the form of a letter of credit or other financial instrument.

setback The distance from a curb, property line, or other reference point within which building is prohibited.

shell space The interior condition of either a new or existing building without improvements or finishes; typically floor, windows, walls, and roof of an enclosed premise; may include some electrical or plumbing improvements, but not demising walls.

site development The installation of all necessary improvements to a site before a building or project can be constructed on the site.

site plan A detailed plan that depicts the location of improvements on a parcel.

soft cost The portion of an equity investment other than the actual cost of the improvements themselves that may be tax-deductible in the first year.

space plan A graphic representation of a tenant's space requirements, showing wall and door locations, room sizes, and sometimes furniture layouts.

special assessment Special charges levied against real property for public improvements that benefit the assessed property.

specific performance When a court requires a defendant to carry out the terms of an agreement or contract.

speculative space (or spec space) Any tenant space that has not been leased before the start of construction on a new building.

stabilized net operating income Projected income less expenses that are subject to change but have been adjusted to reflect equivalent, stable property operations.

stabilized occupancy The optimum range of long-term occupancy that an income-producing real estate project is expected to achieve after exposure for leasing in the open market for a reasonable period of time at terms and conditions comparable to competitive offerings.

Statute of Frauds State law (founded on ancient English law) requiring that certain contracts must be reduced to written form to be enforced by law.

step-up lease (or graduated lease) A lease specifying set increases in rent at set intervals during the term of the lease.

straight lease (fixed lease) A lease specifying a fixed amount of rent that is to be paid periodically, typically monthly, during the entire term of the lease.

strip center Any shopping area that is a row of stores smaller than a neighborhood center anchored by a grocery store.

subcontractor A contractor working under and being paid by the general contractor, often a specialist in nature, such as an electrical contractor or cement contractor.

sublessee A person or identity to whom the rights of use and occupancy under a lease have been conveyed, while the original lessee retains primary responsibility for the obligations of the lease.

subletting The leasing of space from one tenant to another tenant.

subordination agreement An agreement by which the tenant agrees to the priority of a mortgage over the leasehold interest or other claim held by the tenant on the property.

substantial completion The point during construction when the contractor is ready to turn over the property to the tenant or client for acceptance and final punch list, usually on the issuance of a certificate of occupancy.

surety Third party who voluntarily becomes obligated for the debt or obligation of another.

surface rights A right or easement granted with mineral rights, enabling the possessor of the mineral rights to drill or mine through the surface.

survey The process by which a parcel is measured and its boundaries and contents ascertained.

syndicate A partnership organized for participation in a real estate venture. Partners may be limited or unlimited in their liability. (See real estate syndicate.)

synthetic lease (or off-balance-sheet lease) A transaction that appears as a lease from an accounting standpoint but as a loan from a tax standpoint.

take-out loan The loan arranged by the owner or builder developer for a buyer. The construction loan made for construction of the improvements is usually paid in full from the proceeds of this more permanent mortgage loan.

taking A common synonym for condemnation or any interference with private property rights, but it is not essential that there be physical seizure or appropriation.

tax base The assessed valuation of all real property that lies within a taxing authority's jurisdiction. When multiplied by the tax rate, it determines the amount of tax due.

tax lien A statutory lien for nonpayment of property taxes that attaches only to the property upon which the taxes are unpaid.

tax roll A list of the descriptions of all land parcels located within the county, the names of the owners or those receiving the tax bill, assessed values, and tax amounts.

tenancy by entireties An estate that exists only between husband and wife. Each has equal right of enjoyment and possession during their joint lives, and each has the right of survivorship.

tenancy in common Ownership of property by two or more individuals, each of whom has an undivided interest, without the right of survivorship.

tenant (or lessee) One who rents real estate from another and holds an estate by virtue of a lease.

tenant improvement (TI) Improvements made to the leased premises by or for a tenant.

tenant improvement (TI) allowance Defines the fixed amount of money contributed by the landlord toward tenant improvements. The tenant pays any costs that exceed this amount.

tenant mix A phrase used to describe the quality of a property's income stream. In multitenanted properties, institutional investors typically prefer a mixture of national credit tenants, regional credit tenants, and local noncredit tenants.

tenant representation (or buyer's broker) Arrangement whereby a prospective tenant engages a real estate broker as its exclusive agent in negotiating a lease for commercial space.

tenant's use clause Lease language that specifies the business activities the tenant will engage in at the leased premises.

time is of the essence A condition of a contract expressing the essential nature of performance of the contract by a party in a specified period of time.

title The means whereby the owner has the just and full possession of real property.

title insurance A policy issued by a title company that insures against loss resulting from defects of title to a specifically described parcel of real property or from enforcement of liens existing against it at the time the title policy is issued.

title search A review of all recorded documents affecting a specific piece of property to determine the present condition of title.

total assets The sum of all gross investments, cash and equivalents, receivables, and other assets presented on the balance sheet.

total commitment The full mortgage loan amount that is obligated to be funded if all stated conditions are met.

total inventory The total square footage of a type of property within a geographical area, whether vacant or occupied.

total retail area Total floor area of a retail center less common areas. It is the area from which sales are generated and includes any department stores or other areas (such as banks, restaurants, or service stations) not owned by the center.

trade fixtures Personal property that is attached to a structure that is used in the business. Because this property is part of the business and not deemed to be part of the real estate, it is typically removable upon lease termination. It should be defined as such in the lease contract.

triple net lease A lease that requires the tenant to pay all expenses of the property being leased in addition to rent. Typical expenses covered in such a lease include taxes, insurance, maintenance, and utilities.

turnkey project The construction of a project in which a third party (often a contractor) is responsible for the total completion of a building or for the construction of tenant improvements to the customized requirements and specifications of a future owner or tenant.

under construction The period of time after construction has started but before the certificate of occupancy has been issued.

under contract The period of time after a seller has accepted a buyer's offer to purchase a property and during which the buyer performs due diligence and finalizes financing arrangements. During this time, the seller is precluded from entertaining offers from other buyers.

underwriter A company, usually an investment banking firm, that guarantees or participates in a guarantee that an entire issue of stocks or bonds will be purchased.

unencumbered Property that is free of liens and other encumbrances.

unimproved land Most commonly, land without improvements or buildings but also can mean land in its natural state.

unit-in-place method The cost of erecting a building by estimating the cost of each component part (foundations, floors, walls, windows, ceilings, roofs, and so on), including labor and overhead.

usable square footage The area contained within the demising walls of the tenant space that equals the net square footage multiplied by the circulation factor.

use The specific purpose for which a parcel or a building is intended to be used or for which it has been designed or arranged.

vacancy factor The amount of gross revenue that pro forma income statements anticipate will be lost because of vacancies, often expressed as a percentage of the total rentable square footage available in a building or project.

vacancy rate The total amount of available space compared with the total inventory of space and expressed as a percentage.

vacant space Existing tenant space currently being marketed for lease, excluding space available for sublease.

valuation Estimated price, value, or worth. Also, the act of identifying a property's worth via an appraisal.

variable rate (or adjustable rate) A loan interest rate that varies over the term of the loan, usually tied to a predetermined index.

variance Permission for a property owner to depart from the literal requirements of a zoning ordinance that, because of special circumstances, causes a unique hardship.

waiver (for example, lien waiver) The intentional relinquishment or abandonment of a specific claim, privilege, or right.

white box (or vanilla box) The interior condition of a new or existing building or suite with improvements limited to heating and cooling with delivery systems, lighting, electrical switches and outlets, lavatories, a finished ceiling, walls that are prepped for painting, and a concrete slab floor.

work letter An amount of money that a landlord agrees to spend on and the conditions of the construction of the interior of a space per the lease, usually negotiated.

yield The effective return on an investment, as paid in dividends or interest.

yield maintenance premium A penalty, paid by the borrower, designed to make investors whole in the event of early redemption of principal.

zoning The division of a city or town into zones and the application of regulations having to do with the architectural design and structural and intended uses of buildings within such zones.

zoning ordinance The set of laws and regulations controlling the use of land and construction of improvements in a given area or zone.

Index

Printed and bound by CPI Group (UK) Ltd, Croydon, CR0 4YY

23/04/2025